ALCOHOL INTOXICATION: PSYCHIATRIC, PSYCHOLOGICAL, FORENSIC ISSUES

Eric W. Fine, M.D., M.R.C. Psych.

Copyright © 1996 ACFP Press
P.O. Box 5870, Balboa Island, California 92662
All rights reserved
Printed in the United States of America

Alcohol Intoxication: Psychiatric, Psychological, Forensic Issues

ISBN 0-935645-07-1

CONTENTS

I am deeply indebted to my wife Stephanie
for her support and assistance with the manuscript,
and to Anne Ferrarelli for typing this material.

FOREWORD

Eric Fine has written a clear and highly informative book about alcoholism using both his extensive clinical and forensic knowledge and experience. For those who practice forensic psychiatry, this volume contains a comprehensive review of history, case presentation, and topics which will not only enlighten but will be extremely useful in your practice. For clinicians, there is also significant value. The review of pharmacology, symptomatology, and diagnostic criteria is very lucid and will be of great help in the care of patients with either primary alcoholic disease or dual diagnoses.

Alcoholism is a biopsychosocial condition. The debate over how much is genetic versus how much is learned behavior is currently unsolved. There are clearly genetic and cultural factors which predispose people to both use and abuse of alcohol. The biological factors described by Dr. Fine reflect the latest discoveries about blood chemistry and neurotransmitters. The psychological problems which lead a person to drink excessively are also important considerations in developing a full understanding of the disease. Drinking as a defense against depression as well as a form of self-medication are well-recorded phenomena. The cultural and interpersonal issues around drinking all forms of alcohol have been so incorporated into our social fabric that they are hardly considered or are taken for granted in any attempt to understand the condition of alcoholism. Being part of the crowd, one of the boys, or as a rite of passage are common rationalizations. Yet the impact of such activity on susceptible young people, men and women, is considerable. Any understanding of a person with the problem of alcoholism must include all three aspects of mental illness: the biological, the psychological, and the sociocultural. The excellent case histories in Chapters 7 and 8 bear this out.

When I was an intern I wanted to teach myself how to do hypnosis. On the medical ward there was a young black man with a serious stomach ulcer. During his third week (!!!) in the hospital I was able to hypnotize him daily and help him to stop drinking. His history revealed that he drank approximately one bottle of wine every night. The underlying dynamics revealed a very shy and socially frightened fellow who could only participate in social activities with his male friends if he was disinhibited by alcohol. The hypnotic work was twofold: building his self-esteem and a post-hypnotic suggestion that alcohol, specifically wine, would make him sick. He was complete dry for the entire year that I was able to follow him. In this patient, the psychological issues were primary. Clearly, there are analogous cases in which either or all of the other dimensions are most important.

Dr. Fine reviews the relationship between alcoholism and violence very thoroughly. Domestic violence is a problem which is often complicated by alcohol as is street violence. With the increase in the firearm capability of Americans, this is becoming as big a problem as drunk driving or other accidents involving alcohol intoxication. There is a desperate need for this nation to reduce the amount of domestic and street violence. The increasing number of casualties and the pervasive fear in the community are clearly out of control. Gaining some control over excessive use of alcohol would be a valuable contribution to our struggle to reduce violence in our homes and our communities.

A book dedicated to the subject of alcohol and alcoholism is an important addition to the literature. Eric Fine has done a splendid job in preparing this very useful and thoughtful volume.

Paul Jay Fink, M.D.

Dr. Fink, Past President of the American Psychiatric Association (APA), serves as a member of its Board of Trustees. He is currently Senior Consultant to Charter Fairmount Behavioral Health System and a professor in the Department of Psychiatry at Temple University School of Medicine. He is the founder and director of the Einstein Center for the Study of Violence. Dr. Fink has written over 140 articles published on topics that include human sexuality, psychiatric education, economic problems facing modern psychiatry, and on issues concerning violence, parenting and child development. He is co-editor of the book, *The Stigma of Mental Illness*.

INTRODUCTION

Since the dawn of recorded history, societies have used alcoholic beverages in spite of the variety of adverse consequences recognized to be associated with their use. Alcohol is truly an ancient drug and the presence of beer and wine can be found in the archaeological records of the oldest civilizations and in the diet of most primitive peoples. Until the development of distillation in Europe in the 15th century, alcoholic beverages were made by fermentation and consisted of wines and beers with no more than about 14% alcohol. Distilled spirits containing 50% or more of alcohol became available and gained immediate acceptance by those individuals who desired a quicker and more potent effect. The use of alcohol progressed from religious ritual to all elements of societal behavior, becoming the primary drug of abuse in American society, which continues to pay a tremendous price whether measured in dollars, disease, death, violence or shattered lives.

To this day, alcohol abuse and alcoholism remain serious public health problems in the United States and other countries. It is reliably estimated that between ten and eleven million adults in the United States exhibit signs and symptoms of alcohol dependence, and an additional seven to eight million can be categorized as alcohol abusers who do not show signs or symptoms of dependence. Projections for the year 1995 suggest that over eleven million Americans will exhibit signs of alcoholism or alcohol dependence and it is unlikely that the size of the group of alcohol abusers will change appreciably.

The words of Franklin D. Clum, M.D. in his book entitled *Inebriety: Its Causes, Its Results, Its Remedy* (1), published in 1892 are still relevant today.

"Intemperance in the past has disgraced the palace and crown of the prince, the ermine of the judge, the sword of the chieftain, and the miter of the priest. Today it feasts alike upon the innocency of childhood, the beauty of youth, the amiableness of women, the talents of the great, and the experience of age... The time has come for a study of inebriety from a medical stand-point, and when it is treated as a special disease its curability will be found equal to any other disease."

Controversy still exists concerning the concept of alcohol dependence as a disease entity, and we still struggle to unravel the complexities and uncertainties surrounding the study and understanding of alcohol abuse and alcoholism. Many of the problems in the field are semantic and definitional, but there is a current, helpful conceptual framework designed to clarify what is meant by the terms, alcoholism and alcohol abuse. Three different types of drinkers are now recognized; the first group is composed of the majority of adults who drink alcohol with few, if any, problems; the second, (alcohol-abusers), comprises problem drinkers who are not dependent on alcohol, and the third group consists of individuals who are alcohol-dependent and who suffer from the disorder known as alcoholism or alcohol dependence. This relatively simple framework is particularly advantageous for the field of forensic psychiatry where concordance on definitions is clearly of great importance.

Alcohol consumption in the United States increased during the 1960s and 1970s, while the 1980s have been characterized by a gradual decrease in consumption. There also appears to be some evidence of increased abstention from alcohol, especially among men, and adolescents have also decreased their alcohol consumption. Unfortunately, an increase in proportion of heavy drinkers has been noted among young people in their twenties and some increase in the prevalence of alcoholism problems. The major part of the decrease in alcohol consumption is in the drinking of hard liquor, which is the lowest level for spirits since 1958. Consumption of wine and beer remain at about the same level.

Encouraging as these trends might be, there is no reason to suppose that alcohol will not continue to be very frequently used and abused, and the problems of intoxication continue to be challenges for society, with attendant consequences that impact on the fields of forensic psychiatry and psychology.

This book is intended to provide the reader with the most current information regarding the pharmacology of alcohol, the phenomena of intoxication and tolerance, and the adverse consequences of alcohol abuse and alcoholism as they impact on those areas of importance to the forensic psychiatrist. It is anticipated that it will be of value to forensic psychiatrists, attorneys and other behavioral scientists involved in those areas at the interface of psychiatry and the law.

Eric W. Fine, M.D., M.R.C. Psych.

1

PHARMACOLOGY OF ETHYL ALCOHOL

Pharmacologically, ethyl alcohol is included in the group of aliphatic narcotics capable of producing coma. Although the actual mechanisms of how alcohol affects the brain is still uncertain, methods are now becoming available in neuroscience research, which are helping to explore such complex phenomena as alcohol intoxication, tolerance and dependence. It is hoped that these studies will eventually clarify the effects of alcohol in terms of the chemical messenger systems involved in the mediation of the action of alcohol, the so-called receptive areas for alcohol in nerve cell membranes, and the specific behaviors associated with these changes in brain chemistry and physiology.

Following the ingestion of alcohol, absorption occurs from the stomach and small intestine into the bloodstream, from which molecules cross into the brain where they interact with brain cell membranes. Unlike opiates and many other drugs which affect the brain by interacting with specific protein receptors in the brain cell membrane, the action of alcohol is less well understood. It has been proposed in the "membrane hypothesis" that alcohol alters the properties of the lipid components of the brain cell membranes, thus changing membrane fluidity. This might help to explain how very high doses of alcohol produce euphoria, and a reduction in anxiety at lower doses has recently been shown to be related to specific receptive areas within the brain cell membrane; some membrane proteins appear to be particularly sensitive to alcohol.

Many other interesting areas of research are being pursued, including the interaction of alcohol with gamma-aminobutyric acid (GABA) which is the major inhibitory neurotransmitter in the brain, another neurotransmitter receptor system, the glutamate system, and the cyclic adenosine monophosphate system. Also, alcohol has been found to potentiate the effects of somatostatin, a neuropeptide found in the hypothalamus, and this might provide further insight into some aspects of the action of alcohol.

Regardless of these specific neurophysiologic theories of its actions, the effects of alcohol on the individual are well described. It is important to recognize however that there is a wide diversity of response that depends on several factors. For example, the personality of the individual, the specific "mindset," as well as the "setting" in which alcohol is consumed can all influence the types of response that are observed. Alcohol first affects the central nervous system by depressing the reticular activating system and, as a result, the integrating control of the higher brain centers is released. The first mental processes to be affected are those that depend on training and previous experience, and that usually make for sobriety and self restraint. Discriminatory abilities, memory, concentration and insight are first blunted and are ultimately lost. There is an initial increase in confidence, mood changes become uncontrolled and emotional outbursts can occur. These psychic changes usually are accompanied by sensory and motor disturbances.

TOLERANCE

The repeated use of alcohol and other drugs results in the development of tolerance, so that larger doses must be taken in order to produce characteristic effects. This change in sensitivity of the brain is a very general phenomenon seen with a large variety of substances and incorporates many independent mechanisms. Physical dependence does not invariably occur in every situation where tolerance develops.

As well as innate tolerance to alcohol and various other drugs, there are three varieties of acquired tolerance:

1) Dispositional tolerance occurs as a result of changes in the pharmacokinetic properties of the drug in the body so that reduced concentrations exist at the site of action. The most common mechanism is an increased rate of metabolism. It does not result in more than a threefold decrease in sensitivity.

2) Pharmacodynamic tolerance results from adaptive changes within affected systems, so that there is a reduced response in the presence of the same drug concentration.

3) Behavioral tolerance is the change in response to a drug due to behavioral mechanisms. Tolerance develops more rapidly and to a greater extent when the effect of the drug impairs the capacity of the individual to earn a reward or to avoid punishment.

It is usually the case that several different types of tolerance operate together. Tolerance to the effects of alcohol is a very complicated phenomenon, probably involving several neural systems, including the adenylate cyclase and arginine vasopressin systems. Also, several other neurotransmitter systems such as gamma-aminobutyric acid and N-methyl-D-aspartate have been shown to modify their activity in response to chronic alcohol exposure. It has also been shown that chronic exposure to alcohol alters properties of membrane-related bilayers in the brain.

The scientific basis for the phenomenon of tolerance to alcohol, and many other drugs, is well established, and it has important implications in explaining behavior that is related to intoxication with alcohol. In forensic psychiatry, it is particularly important in helping to qualify opinions regarding the behavior that would be expected with known blood alcohol concentrations.

Although tolerance to alcohol and other drugs does not necessarily influence the likelihood of repeated use, it often affects patterns of use because the desired effect, for example, euphoria, can only be obtained by increasing the amount of alcohol consumed. The need for increased quantities of alcohol might well increase the risk of toxic effects. The chronic use of alcohol results in an increased rate of alcohol metabolism, as well as a pharmacodynamic tolerance, but there is no significant elevation of the lethal dose, and severe acute intoxication sometimes with marked respiratory depression, can coincide with chronic alcohol intoxication. Pharmacodynamic tolerance in the central nervous system, or more rapid metabolism, can contribute to cross-tolerance between alcohol and other drugs. Tolerance to alcohol usually produces cross-tolerance to general anesthetics, benzodiazepines, opioids and other sedative-hypnotics.

PHYSICAL DEPENDENCE ON ALCOHOL

Chronic, regular use of alcohol, usually in large doses, results in high concentrations of alcohol in the blood being maintained and this produces clinically significant physical dependence on alcohol. The body is capable of metabolizing approximately one oz (30 cc) of whiskey in an hour, and theoretically if one such drink was taken per hour over the course of the day, there would be no substantial increase in blood alcohol concentration. However, only slightly larger amounts of alcohol, for example, 4 oz of whiskey every three hours, will produce much higher blood alcohol concentrations. This can result in significant physical dependence developing in only a matter of days.

Physical dependence on alcohol is characterized by withdrawal symptoms that usually appear within twelve to seventy-two hours after ceasing drinking. It has also been noted that a relative decline in blood alcohol concentration may precipitate a withdrawal syndrome, so that it is possible for withdrawal symptoms to be present with an appreciably high blood alcohol. With even low degrees of dependence on alcohol, the withdrawal syndrome is characterized by disturbed sleep, weakness, anxiety and mild tremor that lasts for a short period.

When dependence is severe, the withdrawal syndrome is equally so. The original description of this syndrome by Victor and Adams (2) over forty years ago, remains the basis for the recognition of three rather distinct withdrawal states: the tremulous syndrome, alcohol-related seizure disorder, and delirium tremens. In clinical practice, there is a great degree of overlapping of these three states. A state of tremulousness appears within a few hours after the last drink and is often accompanied by weakness, profuse perspiration and anxiety. There may be nausea and vomiting and there is almost always hyperreflexia. The tremor can range in severity from mild to extremely severe and visual hallucinations occur, first only with the eyes closed, but later while the eyes are open. This stage is sometimes referred to as acute alcoholic hallucinosis, but it should be noted that hallucinations are sometimes reported when alcoholics are severely intoxicated. Occurrence of grand mal seizures is not as common in alcohol withdrawal states as in barbiturate withdrawal.

A state of tremor usually reaches its maximum intensity within 24 to 48 hours, and if seizures occur, they are most likely within the first 24 hours after ceasing drinking. As the syndrome worsens, there is confusion, disorientation and agitation. The hallucinations often become persecutory and extremely vivid. These symptoms usually occur on about the third withdrawal day and this state of tremulous delirium was first described by Thomas Sutton in 1813 (3). Complications include hyperthermia, exhaustion and cardiovascular collapse. The withdrawal syndrome is usually self-limited and if the patient does not die, full recovery occurs within 5 to 7 days without any treatment.

Alcohol withdrawal syndromes have been seen in babies born to alcoholic mothers, and characteristic anatomical changes have been described that constitute a fetal alcohol syndrome. Chronic alcoholic patients frequently suffer from nutritional deficiencies, nutritional amblyopia, Wernicke's encephalopathy and Korsakoff's psychosis. These conditions are thought to be caused by secondary nutritional deficiencies, while fatty liver, liver cirrhosis, cardiomyopathy and skeletal muscle disease are probably due to direct toxic effects of alcohol. Cerebral atrophy has been demonstrated to occur much more frequently than first thought in chronic alcoholic patients and several studies suggest that the degree of cerebral atrophy is related to the duration and intensity of exposure to alcohol.

As well as their obvious clinical significance, the presence of many of these conditions has special relevance for the field of forensic psychiatry.

THE EFFECTS OF ALCOHOL ON THE CENTRAL NERVOUS SYSTEM

The medical consequences of consuming alcohol, usually in large quantities, are well known. They include effects on the gastrointestinal tract, alcohol-induced liver disorders, nutritional and metabolic disorders, and effects on the cardiovascular system. There are also effects on the immune system, and endocrine and reproductive functions can also be influenced by alcohol.

Alcohol acts as a primary and continuous central nervous system depressant, and any apparent stimulation is thought to result from the activity of those parts of the brain that have been freed from inhibitory control as a result of the depression by alcohol of the inhibitory control mechanisms. The parts of the brain involved in the most highly integrated functions are first affected, with the reticular activating system and certain sites in the cerebral cortex being particularly susceptible. As a result of the cortical centers losing their integrating control, thought processes and judgment are initially affected, followed by disruption of motor processes. Those processes that depend on training and previous experience are affected first so that sobriety and self-restraint are lost. There is a false sense of confidence, speech may become more eloquent initially, and there are frequent emotional outbursts and uncontrolled mood swings.

It should be emphasized that alcohol generally increases neither mental nor physical abilities, although it is common for the individual to believe that his performance is improved. In fact, sophisticated psychometric testing has shown that efficiency is decreased. There are however, some unusual circumstances where alcohol may cause some improvement. One example is where inhibitory control is so great that it prevents the individual from carrying out a task at which he would be normally skilled. Under this circumstance, moderate quantities of alcohol might allow that person to function somewhat more effectively.

The effects of alcohol on the central nervous system are generally proportional to the concentration of alcohol in the blood, with effects tending to be more pronounced when the concentration is rising than when it is falling. Alcohol is a poor general anesthetic because there is very little margin between the anesthetic dose and that which depresses respiration. It has analgesic properties, and 50 cc of 95% alcohol will raise the pain threshold between 35% to 40%. It also causes a measure of euphoria which can produce a degree of relative detachment from pain, much like opiates.

2

BLOOD ALCOHOL CONCENTRATION

Alcohol is generally absorbed from the stomach and small intestine, although absorption can occur very rapidly through the lungs. There have been cases of fatal intoxication as a result of such inhalation. Absorption from the stomach is at first rapid, but then decreases markedly, although the gastric concentration is still high. Major influences on absorption rate include volume, character and dilution of the alcoholic beverage, presence of food in the stomach, and the time taken to ingest the drink, as well as individual variations. Complete absorption may require anywhere between two to six hours and most foods in the stomach will delay absorption. Beer exerts some retarding action on absorption, much like that of food. Alcohol is absorbed from the small intestine extremely rapidly and completely, and this probably explains why patients who have undergone gastrectomies become intoxicated by lesser quantities of alcohol. The time of gastric emptying, and therefore the phase of extremely rapid intestinal absorption, is probably the main factor in determining the variety of rates of absorption seen in different individuals under different circumstances.

Ninety to 98% of the alcohol that is absorbed is completely oxidized, chiefly in the liver by alcohol dehydrogenase, to acetaldehyde. The acetaldehyde is converted to acetyl coenzyme A, which is further oxidized through the citric acid cycle or utilized in various anabolic reactions. About 2% of the alcohol escapes oxidation and most is excreted through the kidneys and lungs, with very small amounts found in sweat, tears, bile and saliva.

The measurement of alcohol in various body fluids is frequently important for medicolegal purposes. The concentration of alcohol in the blood can be determined directly, or it can be estimated from the concentration either in expired air, which is about 0.05% that in blood, or less frequently, in the urine which is about 130% of that in the blood.

The relationship between the blood alcohol concentration and clinical signs and symptoms is of great medicolegal importance. As the concentration of alcohol in the blood rises, there is a corresponding increase in the number and severity of the signs and symptoms of intoxication. As stated previously, these changes are more marked when the concentrations are rising than when falling. It should be emphasized that the particular effects reported to occur at different blood alcohol concentrations are subject to sometimes marked individual differences.

Most of the reactions described in the literature for the different blood alcohol concentrations are based on so-called moderate drinkers who have been drinking for a few years. The phenomenon known as tolerance has already been described, and this can influence the reactions at varying blood alcohol concentrations to a significant degree. Thus, for an individual who has been drinking large quantities of alcohol for many years, the reactions would generally be of lesser magnitude at each concentration than they would be for the so-called average drinker. It is well recognized that many alcoholic individuals are able to consume over a quart of whiskey daily without showing pronounced signs of intoxication. Some of these individuals are also able to perform complex laboratory tasks at blood alcohol concentrations much higher than those that would have produced quite severe behavioral disturbances in non-addicted drinkers.

There are also differences in reaction to alcohol within the individual, who at one time might appear intoxicated with two drinks, while on other occasions might need four drinks to appear equally intoxicated. Precisely what accounts for these differences is not known, but it is well recognized that alcohol may on one occasion bring relief from anxiety and at other times have no effect whatsoever, or even intensify this symptom. The physical and emotional state of the individual at the time the alcohol is consumed will determine, to some extent, the degree of manifest intoxication.

Having said that, however, there is general agreement that threshold effects, for example, increased reaction time, diminished fine motor control and impaired judgment, appear when the concentration of alcohol in the blood is .02% to .03%. Also, approximately 50% of persons show obvious signs of intoxication when the blood alcohol concentration is .15%. In those persons who die as a result of acute alcohol intoxication, the average blood alcohol concentration is .40%.

Table 1 is a modification of that of Kurt M. Dubowski, Ph.D. (4) who summarized the correlation between blood alcohol concentrations and clinical signs and symptoms. It is important to note that the stated categories overlap and therefore the signs and symptoms found in these categories also overlap. Useful guidelines are provided for the behaviors that can generally be expected within the range of blood alcohol concentrations shown.

There is substantial epidemiologic evidence that demonstrates a positive correlation between alcohol intoxication and accidents. The effect of alcohol on driving-related skills has received specific attention and it has been clearly demonstrated that even small doses of alcohol can result in significant impairment in the ability to operate a motor vehicle, and presumably other forms of transportation.

Accurate vision is obviously a very important factor in operating an automobile safely. Objects must not only be clearly seen, but the eyes must also be able to focus on objects in the visual field for short periods, and then track them as the vehicle moves. Blood alcohol concentrations (BAC) as low as .03% to .05% are shown to interfere with voluntary movements of the eyes and significantly impair the ability to accurately track a moving target. Eye-hand movements and reaction times, along with the brain's control of eye movements, influence the complex task of steering an automobile. Steering ability begins to show impairment at BACs between .03% and .04%. Paying attention to road signs, responding to traffic signals, as well as other cues are critical in the safe operation of a motor vehicle.

At about .04% BAC (representing two drinks consumed in about one hour by a 150-lb man) narrowing of the attentional field begins to be evident, and this rapidly increases as the blood alcohol concentration rises.

Table 1. Correlation Between Blood Alcohol Concentrations and Clinical Signs

BLOOD ALCOHOL CONCENTRATION (BAC)	USUAL CLINICAL SICNS AND SYMPTOMS
1. 0 - 0.06%	No apparent influence. Behavior normal by ordinary observation. Slight changes detectable by special tests.
2. 0.03% - 0.12%	Mild euphoria, sociability, talkativeness, increased self-confidence, decreased inhibitions. Diminution of attention, judgment and control. Loss of efficiency in finer performance tests.
3. 0.09% - 0.25%	Emotional instability; decreased inhibitions, loss of critical judgment. Impairment of memory and comprehension. Decreased sensitory response; increased reaction time. Some muscular incoordination.
4. 0.18% - 0.30%	Disorientation, mental confusion; dizziness. Exaggerated emotional states (fear, anger, grief, etc.) Disturbance of sensation (diplopia, etc.) and of perceptions of color, form, motion, dimensions. Decreased pain sense. Impaired balance, muscular incoordination, staggering gait, slurred speech.
5. 0.27% - 0.40%	Apathy, general inertia, approaching paralysis, Markedly decreased response to stimuli. Marked muscular incoordination, inability to stand or walk. Vomiting, incontinence of urine and feces. Impaired consciousness, sleep or stupor.
6. 0.35% - 0.50%	Complete unconsciousness, coma, anesthesia. Depressed or abolished reflexes, subnormal temperature. Incontinence of urine and feces, embarrassment of circulation and respiration. Possible death.
7. 0.45% and above	Death may ensue from respiratory paralysis.

To operate a motor vehicle safely, the driver must constantly monitor a rapidly changing situation so that the vehicle remains in the correct direction and lane while attention is paid to traffic signals, pedestrians, and other vehicles. There is therefore a need to be able to divide attention among different skills and behaviors, and it has been demonstrated that alcohol-impaired drivers are unable to adequately divide their attention between several tasks, but tend to favor one of them. There is a marked tendency for intoxicated drivers to overconcentrate on steering the vehicle while they become much less vigilant with regard to other safety information. A blood alcohol concentration as low as .02% (approximately one drink) has been shown to result in divided attention deficits.

The results of experimental studies on the effects of alcohol on driving performance continually demonstrate that even one or two drinks can adversely affect certain skills that are important for safely operating a motor vehicle. As the blood alcohol concentration rises, the degree of alcohol-related impairment increases and at any given blood alcohol concentration, some skills are more impaired than others. The complexity of the task involved, as well as the blood alcohol concentration, influence the degree of the impairment.

The degree of impairment associated with a particular blood alcohol concentration is not constant and can vary between individuals. More experienced drinkers tend to show less impairment than less experienced drinkers in tests of motor coordination, sensory perception and intellectual function due to tolerance. Younger drivers tend to have little experience with driving and drinking, and are therefore at greater risk. Many states have adopted lower blood alcohol concentrations to establish legal intoxication in minors. Conversely, older drivers (above the age of sixty-nine) have higher degrees of alcohol-related impairment at given blood alcohol concentrations.

There are several important issues that need to be considered so far as forensic psychiatry and blood alcohol concentrations are concerned. Traffic safety and law enforcement require accurate measurements of impairment, but the devices used in the laboratory to measure impairment are impractical for use at the roadside. It is for this reason that all states have enacted laws which assume that a blood alcohol concentration above a specified limit is sufficient evidence of impairment for legal purposes. The laws are based on the assumption that the blood alcohol concentration alone is an accurate indicator of impairment. In the field of alcohol highway safety, the BAC is usually determined by measurement of the alcohol concentration in the breath using a hand-held device. This procedure must be performed correctly with an accurately calibrated instrument, and does represent an accurate blood alcohol concentration without any interference from alcohol vapors contaminating the mouth.

The blood alcohol concentration at the time of the accident is often not known, but needs to be calculated from a sample of breath or blood tested for alcohol at a later time. This might be several hours after the accident, when the blood alcohol concentration may be much lower than at the time of the accident itself. In such cases, the BAC at the time of the accident is calculated based on standard equations of the rate at which alcohol is metabolized by the body. Elimination of alcohol is, however, influenced by several factors and can vary significantly from person to person or in the same individual at different times. These calculations based on an average elimination rate for populations can give rise to considerable error when applied to individuals.

Although the BAC is "frozen" at the time of death, the measurement of the BAC in post-mortem specimens is complicated by the presence of alcohol produced by microbial fermentation. The most effective way to minimize this problem is to analyze the alcohol content of the liquid that is present in the eyeball behind the lens (the vitreous humor). The alcohol concentration in vitreous humor is commonly used to confirm post-mortem BAC measurements, as this liquid is protected from microbial activity. When blood is obtained from the heart or other body cavities after death, the BAC is often artificially high.

Estimates of the BAC can be made if the number and type of drinks consumed, the body weight and sex of the individual, and the time spent drinking are known. Reports of alcohol concentrations sometimes refer to *serum* alcohol concentrations which are approximately 15% greater than BACs. Conversions, therefore, must be made to the *blood* alcohol concentration before an opinion is given as to the consequences of the BAC.

Drinks contain different amounts of alcohol so it is important to know whether the person has consumed regular beer, light beer, 100 proof spirits, 80 proof spirits, or wines which contain between 12% and 20% alcohol. The same amount of alcohol will be present in four 12-oz bottles of regular beer, five 12-oz light beers, four and one-half drinks containing one oz of 100 proof spirits, approximately 7 oz of 60 proof spirits, and 19 oz of 12% wine. In practice it is common for various combinations of such drinks to be consumed at varying rates, and BACs obtained in this manner are only estimates.

Each ounce of alcohol contributes approximately .02% to the BAC, while alcohol is metabolized at an average rate of .018% per hour, with a range of .015% to .02% per hour. Individual absorption and metabolism rates vary quite considerably, and other variables include the rate of consumption, presence of food in the stomach, type of beverage and, most importantly, body mass. Thus, five 12-oz light beers consumed over an hour will result in a BAC of approximately .09% in a 180-lb man, while the same quantity will produce a BAC of about .11% in a man weighing 150 lbs. A female weighing 110 lbs who consumed this quantity of beer will have a BAC of approximately .18%. Using similar mathematics an estimation of alcohol present in the body can be calculated from a known BAC concentration.

Estimation of the BAC at times before or after that already known is based on knowledge of the time the last drink was consumed and the rate at which alcohol is metabolized. The latter is subject to considerable variation so that these estimates are open to serious criticism and cross-examination in court. The estimate has more validity if the time sought is several hours after termination of drinking.

It is possible to arrive at these estimates using rather sophisticated mathematical formulae but easily available and simple slide rules (Alco-calculators) make the task a great deal easier and are just as reliable.

3

ALCOHOL ABUSE
AND ALCOHOL DEPENDENCE

Alcohol abuse and alcohol dependence (alcoholism) have been shown to be two quite distinct forms of problematic drinking, both of which produce adverse social and medical consequences. Alcohol dependence is characterized by phenomena such as craving, physical dependence and tolerance, with an impairment in the ability to refrain from drinking alcohol. Alcohol abuse occurs when non-dependent individuals consume large quantities of alcohol with resulting health problems and/or social/legal complications. Approximately 10% of adult Americans are affected by the two problem drinking patterns, which as well as producing problems for the drinker, result in secondary problems for families of the drinker and other members of society with whom the drinker comes into contact.

Although the causes of alcohol dependence are poorly understood, it is an almost classic example of a biopsychosocial disorder. Alcohol is still used by more Americans than any other drug, including tobacco products. Racial and ethnic groups in the United States have been shown to have different alcohol use patterns and risk for alcohol-related problems. Also, drinking problems and heavy consumption of alcohol are clearly associated with being male, young, and single.

Alcohol dependence has been found to run in families and there is some evidence, although not too convincing, that there might be genetic transmission of vulnerability for the more serious forms of alcohol dependence. Drinking behavior is certainly influenced by ethnic and cultural factors and it is likely that gene-environment interactions are important in the etiology of alcohol dependence.

Sociopsychological factors are clearly of great importance in the causation of alcohol abuse and alcohol dependence. The psychological state of the drinker, especially regarding expectations about the effects of alcohol, as well as the pharmacologic effects of the drug, are involved in the transition from social drinking to problem drinking. Alcohol, as well as some other drugs, initially produces very pleasing effects that reinforce continued consumption. The reduction of anxiety and the production of mild euphoria by alcohol represent powerful reinforcers that probably play a major role in the production of alcohol dependence.

The part played by personality factors in the etiology of alcohol dependence is very controversial; many studies have found a high incidence of sociopathy, depression and low self-esteem in alcoholic patients. Many of these individuals have a significant history of anxiety disorder and/or depression preceding, and continuing in conjunction with, their dependence on alcohol. Attention to, and management of, these coexisting psychiatric states is often the difference between success and failure in attaining and maintaining abstention.

The etiology of alcohol dependence is obviously extremely complex, and it involves a dynamic interplay of biological, psychological and sociocultural factors. Alcoholic patients are members of a diverse, heterogeneous group that probably consists of many sub-groups, with different types of alcohol dependence having different causations, drinking constellations and outcomes. Each individual's history is specific and his or her experiences are unique.

Accurate and reliable criteria for the diagnosis of alcohol dependence are important clinically, particularly when medicolegal issues are involved. Correctly diagnosing alcohol dependence demands a reliable and comprehensive history including the first exposure to alcoholic beverages, the development of specific drinking patterns, and the effects of this drinking on the patient's behavior. A detailed medical history is necessary, as well as a complete physical examination including appropriate laboratory studies, X-rays, computerized axial tomography and magnetic resonance imaging. An independent history obtained from a family member can also be of great value in justifying and supporting the data provided by the patient. This kind of comprehensive evaluation is absolutely essential when testifying to the presence or absence of alcohol dependence in court-related matters.

The *Diagnostic and Statistical Manual of Mental Disorders* (DSM-4) (5) includes alcohol abuse and alcohol dependence in the category of substance use disorders and is the most recent attempt to define these concepts and objectify their diagnosis. Table 2 shows the diagnostic criteria for alcohol dependence. These criteria should be used whenever a diagnosis of alcohol dependence or alcohol abuse is made.

Table 2. Diagnostic Criteria for Alcohol Dependence

A. Either a pattern of pathological alcohol use or impairment in social or occupational functioning due to alcohol use:

Pattern of pathological alcohol use: need for daily use of alcohol for adequate functioning; inability to cut down or stop drinking; repeated efforts to control or reduce excess drinking by "going on the wagon" (periods of temporary abstinence) or restricting drinking to certain times of the day; binges (remaining intoxicated throughout the day for at least two days); occasional consumption of a fifth of spirits or its equivalent in wine or beer); amnesic periods for events occurring while intoxicated (blackouts); continuation of drinking despite a serious physical disorder that the individual knows is exacerbated by alcohol use; drinking of non-beverage alcohol.

Impairment in social or occupational functioning due to alcohol use: e.g., violence while intoxicated, absence from work, loss of job, legal difficulties (e.g., arrest for intoxicated behavior, traffic accidents while intoxicated), arguments or difficulties with family or friends because of excessive alcohol use.

B. Either tolerance or withdrawal:

Tolerance: need for markedly increased amounts of alcohol to achieve the desired effect, or markedly diminished effect with regular use of the same amount.

Withdrawal: development of Alcohol Withdrawal (e.g., morning "shakes" and malaise relieved by drinking) after cessation of or reduction in drinking.

The diagnostic criteria for alcohol dependence include several specific behaviors that have implications for forensic psychiatry. For example, alcohol dependence is characterized by "inability to cut down or stop drinking" and this implies an irresistible urge to drink alcohol and continue to do so. This is a factor that is important to take into consideration when evaluating behavior that has been carried out by the alcohol dependent person. Also of importance are the amnesic periods or alcoholic blackouts that occur during intoxication. The patients claim to have no memory whatsoever for their behavior during these "blackouts," and the issue of responsibility for this behavior is often in question. Similar conditions occur in psychological fugue states and also with psychomotor seizures where the same question for responsibility can be raised.

The diagnostic criteria include impairment in social or occupational functioning due to alcohol abuse and this is often of medicolegal importance. Included here would be violence while intoxicated, arrests for intoxicated behavior, and motor vehicle accidents while intoxicated. Because of the extremely high incidence of alcohol abuse and alcohol dependence in our society, the behaviors associated with alcohol intoxication are major public health problems.

THE DIAGNOSIS OF ALCOHOLISM

In the general field of medical practice there can be few areas worthy of more emphasis than that concerned with diagnosis and evaluation. It is impossible for any treatment approach to be rationally directed without a comprehensive diagnosis, and too many patients, particularly those with alcohol dependency syndromes, continue to be involved with inappropriate attempts at treatment because of the failure to perform a thorough, methodical clinical evaluation.

The field of alcoholism continues to be plagued by the lack of a universally accepted definition of the concept of alcohol dependency, and a persistent, moralistic attitude towards the problem, and the result is often underdiagnosis, but occasionally overdiagnosis. Many attempts have been made to eliminate these biases but none have been totally successful.

A large number of diagnostic screening tests for alcoholism have become popular in recent years. These range from an extensive set of physiological and behavioral criteria for the diagnosis of alcoholism published by the National Council on Alcoholism (6), to Griffith Edwards et al.'s (7) rather tongue-in-cheek, solitary question as to how often a drink in the morning is taken after a night's drinking. Between these two extremes we find Guze et al (8) using a seven-question instrument, Seltzer's (9) brief 25-item Michigan Alcoholism Screening Test, and Mortimer et al.'s (10) self-administered Yes/No Questionnaire, which takes approximately 35 minutes to administer. These and several other questionnaires, which can be found described in the literature, include questions about the quantity and frequency of alcohol intake, about symptoms that indicate loss of control over alcohol consumption, and about various types of problems that can be attributed to drinking, such as marital disharmony, problems at work, driving under the influence, and other related anti-social activity. In screening large populations for the presence of alcoholism these instruments have proved invaluable, and the more comprehensive ones have made possible the detection of milder cases of alcoholism or earlier stages of the disorder. The scales or aforementioned tests have proven to be reliable, efficient, and simple enough to apply, and one or the other should be considered for routine use with populations where alcohol abuse and alcoholism are suspected to be problematic.

Regardless of the screening instrument or questionnaire used, a truly comprehensive and meaningful diagnosis of alcohol dependency must still depend on the acquisition of a reliable, complete history, ideally supplemented by third-party information, and direct clinical observation of the patient. While it is essential to have agreed-upon criteria for the presence of alcohol dependency, it is also critically important to recognize that alcoholism is a complex phenomenon which often occurs in the presence of some type of personality malformation or psychiatric disorder. If treatment of the individual alcoholic patient is to be individually determined a diagnosis of alcohol dependency is not enough. A more meaningful differential diagnosis must take place wherein the specific nature of the alcohol dependency syndrome is elicited to the best of one's ability with the information that is available.

Particularly important in this regard is the identification of clinically significant depression and anxiety. These disorders of affect have been found, usually in combination, in appreciable numbers of alcoholic patients, and it is sometimes uncertain whether they precede, and contribute to the alcoholism, or are secondary results. Attempts to differentiate primary or essential alcoholism from secondary or reactive alcohol dependency are difficult but worthwhile, and should influence the treatment modalities recommended. Diagnosis of the associated psychiatric syndrome should be carried out when the patient has been free from alcohol for a period of time long enough to eliminate the acute effects of the alcohol, but this time period will vary from person to person.

Efforts at diagnosis in general medicine are enhanced by the availability of a wide range of objective measures with which to supplement the clinical history. The use of x-rays, blood and other body fluid examination, electrocardiograms, and electroencephalograms support and refine the physician's diagnostic efforts. Unfortunately, diagnosis of psychiatric syndromes generally remains almost entirely dependent on the history and observation of the patient, and is, therefore, much more controversial and subjective. The diagnosis of alcoholics, particularly, is further complicated by the difficulty in obtaining from patients accurate information regarding their use of alcohol. The underlying dynamics of many forms of alcohol dependency are characterized by conscious lying about drinking because of real or imagined consequences, or by a more subtle process of denial which results in equally unreliable information. The need therefore for accurate biochemical tests to detect alcoholism is obvious.

As indicated in the National Council on Alcoholism's publication "Criteria for the Diagnosis of Alcoholism" (11), the presence of alcohol-related medical disease ranks as a major criterion for the presence of alcoholism. Therefore, no evaluation of alcoholic patients would be acceptable without a complete physical evaluation, including, but not limited to, hematologic studies, uric acid, blood sugar, serum amylase and a battery of liver function tests. The results of such investigations can often provide objective evidence of alcohol-related pathology.

In recent years studies of plasma amino acid metabolism and alcohol have led to the discovery of a biochemical test that is felt to be specific for active alcoholism. This is based on the measurement of plasma alpha-amino-butyric acid relative to leucine. This particular test is promising because it has a minimum of false positive determinations. When used in combination with gamma glutamyl transpeptidase determination, it is reported as providing a sensitive means of detection of alcoholism, and along with other tests of this nature might provide the clinician in the future with more objective support for his diagnosis.

Another measure which is being used to support clinical observations in the diagnosis of alcoholism is the blood alcohol concentration. There is good reason to suppose that any person who has a blood alcohol concentration of 0.15% or higher, in the absence of gross intoxication, has acquired appreciable tolerance to alcohol and in all likelihood is alcohol dependent. The blood alcohol concentration can of course be obtained directly from measurement of the blood, or, more conveniently, by analysis of the breath alcohol. The use of a Breathalyzer in various settings where patients with drinking problems might be encountered, could therefore provide useful information to enable the clinician to make a diagnosis of alcohol dependency. Recommendation should be made for any patient registering a blood alcohol concentration of 0.15% or more to receive a detailed work-up for the presence of alcoholism.

As with many other diseases in medicine generally, and psychiatry in particular, if a high index of suspicion for the presence of a particular disorder is not present, any cases other than the most obvious often remain undiagnosed. It is not uncommon, in a variety of clinical settings, to see patients in whom no adequate drinking history has been taken, and physicians and other personnel involved in evaluating patients must be given the basic knowledge and skills to elicit an accurate and comprehensive alcohol history, supported by as many objective laboratory tests as possible. Further progress in the treatment of alcoholic patients will only occur with increasingly refined and sophisticated delineation of specific alcoholic syndromes, and subgroups within the alcohol dependent population.

4

ALCOHOL AND AGGRESSION

Aggressive behavior and its consequences are manifestly of great importance in forensic psychiatry and psychology. As long as alcohol has existed, intoxication has been associated with violence and aggression. A relationship between violence and other drugs has also been observed, particularly with the amphetamines and phencyclidine. But it is alcohol that is paired with the highest incidence of aggression and violence.

High rates of homicide, suicide and sexual assault have been shown to be associated with acute and chronic alcohol consumption. It has also been stressed that aggressive behavior under the influence of alcohol depends on other associated factors, such as the context in which the drinking occurs, varying cultural drinking patterns, the dosage of alcohol, and the experience of the drinker.

Patients with brain damage exhibit the classical disturbances of emotional lability and loss of control of emotional expression. The former is characterized by rapidly shifting mood with little provocation, and the latter, sometimes called "emotional incompetence," consists of outbursts of crying or laughing in response to minimal stimuli. It has also been recognized that brain damage is associated with impaired control of aggressive behavior, and when this is extreme, one often sees outbursts of uncontrollable violence. Sometimes, this can be shown to be associated with specific cerebral pathology, such as occurs with seizure disorders, some cerebral tumors and other forms of organic brain disease.

In many habitually aggressive individuals however, there are no obvious signs of cerebral disorder, and it has been postulated that in these individuals there may be abnormalities of the neural apparatus controlling aggressive responses. Possible dysfunction of the "limbic brain," and especially of the amygdaloid nuclei within the temporal lobes have been implicated. With animals, aggressive behavior can be facilitated, decreased or abolished by cerebral lesions, mostly situated in or near the limbic system or hypothalamus.

Clinically, a high proportion of patients with temporal lobe epilepsy show explosive aggressive tendencies, often as a persistent trait in their personalities, as well as sometimes occurring in relation to seizures. Also, abnormal outbursts of rage and destructive behavior have been observed in patients with brain tumors. The hypothalamus, hippocampus and amygdaloid nuclei are frequently involved in such tumors. The young man who murdered his mother and wife in August, 1966 and proceeded to the University of Texas tower and killed fourteen people with gunfire was found, at autopsy, to have a glioblastoma multiforme. A lowered threshold for aggression and brain pathology has also been demonstrated in cases of birth trauma, head injuries and intracerebral infections.

It is now well recognized that alcohol has a very damaging effect on the structure of the brain when used in large quantities for long periods of time. This alteration in brain anatomy might well contribute to the aggressive behavior associated with alcohol usage. Acute alcohol intoxication in individuals with pre-existing brain damage, or temporal lobe epilepsy, could serve as a trigger for further reducing the threshold for aggressive behavior.

In recent years, attempts to explain aggressive behavior have moved from the area of brain anatomy to that of neurotransmitter physiology. Many studies in animals have pointed to serotonin playing an important role in the regulation of aggression. Also, studies in humans have shown that low levels of 5-hydroxy indole acetic acid (5-HIAA) are related to suicidal and aggressive behaviors. As 5-HIAA is a metabolite of serotonin, this provides further evidence that this particular neurotransmitter is important in the regulation of aggression.

A significant proportion of alcohol-dependent patients attempt and often succeed in committing suicide. The fact that alcoholic patients have significantly lower levels of serotonin than control subjects matched for age and other variable also provides a link between depressed serotonin levels and, in this case, self-destructive behavior. One study demonstrated that males who attempted murder and also those who succeeded, had lower levels of 5-HIAA in their cerebrospinal fluid than did matched controls (12). Lower 5-HIAA levels have also been found in offenders with impulse control disorder who had a history of attempted suicide compared with a matched group of violent offenders who had no history of attempted suicide (13). As a result of these studies, Roy, et al. (14) have proposed that a disorder of the central serotonin system might characterize a subgroup of alcoholic patients who have an earlier onset of alcohol abuse, violent, impulsive outbursts and a sociopathic personality disorder. It is likely that many other such subgroups in the alcoholic population will be identified in the future with the possibility that specific neurotransmitter defects will be identified.

A possible link between aggression and levels of testosterone has long been proposed, based partly on the observation that males in most cultures tend to be more aggressive and dominant. As it is recognized that alcohol also increases aggressive behavior, attempts have been made to explore what relationships, if any, exist between alcohol and testosterone levels. A recent study by Winslow et al. (15) studied the interactions between testosterone levels, alcohol and aggression in squirrel monkeys. The administration of testosterone for several weeks produced no apparent increase in the baseline aggressiveness of the dominant monkey, although their level of aggression was increased by low doses of alcohol. The submissive monkeys similarly treated with testosterone did show increased aggressiveness when given low doses of alcohol. Previous studies had indicated that the administration of alcohol alone did not trigger this aggressiveness in submissive monkeys, so that testosterone could be considered to have mediated the effect. The proposal has been made that testosterone might well activate some alcohol-sensitive brain mechanisms involved in aggressive behavior.

There is obviously no simple explanation for aggressive behavior and cultural, sociologic, psychologic and biologic factors all play important roles. The place of alcohol in this complex matrix of factors is still poorly understood, but a strong association between alcohol and aggressive behavior is self-evident. The specific role that alcohol plays in any individual case needs to be precisely elicited and its relative importance clearly defined.

A recently published book, *Vessels of Rage Engines of Power*, by James Graham (16), describes in detail many well known historical figures who had suffered from alcoholism and demonstrated behaviors characterized by extreme aggression resulting sometimes in mass murder. Graham's argument for the presence of alcoholism in the many historical figures he describes is convincing, and the relationship between alcohol and aggressive behavior is clearly evident in his description of Joseph Stalin, Alexander the Great, John Wayne Gacy, Jr. and other serial killers. Although the use of alcohol itself might very well result in aggressive behavior, the relationship between alcohol as a drug and aggression is obviously a complex one, and Graham emphasizes that when alcoholics stop drinking, many of their symptoms persist, including a pathological need for power. Graham argues convincingly that the personality traits found in alcoholics produce individuals who have a tremendous need for ego satisfaction, and therefore not only seek power, but also abuse it.

While alcohol can be viewed as a drug capable of producing aggressive behavior, the evidence would suggest that personality factors, perhaps released from inhibitory control by alcohol, are also critically important variables. The presence of aggressive personality traits in many individuals would not themselves result in aggression were it not for associated intoxication with alcohol or other drugs. It is reasonable to suppose that drinking to levels of severe intoxication would be more likely to lead to aggressive behavior than alcohol consumed in relatively small quantities, preferably as part of a meal. Whether or not very small amounts of alcohol can result in severe intoxication in some individuals is still a matter of some controversy. The disorder described as alcohol idiosyncratic intoxication or "pathological intoxication" was included in the *Diagnostic and Statistical Manual of Mental Disorders* (DSM-III) (17), but has been excluded from DSM-IV.

In the opinion of the author, the exclusion of this diagnostic entity is unwise, and is not based on any good scientific information. In clinical practice, it is quite clear that a small, but important number of individuals do indeed become quickly and severely intoxicated with very small quantities of alcohol. Whether or not this is an inherited or acquired disorder is not known, but it is certainly not uncommon for people who have suffered severe head injuries to have a marked lowering of tolerance to alcohol. Encephalitis has also been associated with a temporary or permanent loss of tolerance to alcohol. In spite of DSM-IV's omission of this diagnostic entity, forensic psychiatrists would do well to consider this diagnosis in cases where the history and observation of the individual point in this direction.

5

ALCOHOL AND ACCIDENTS

The role of alcohol in accidents of all kinds is of great medicolegal importance and is a reflection of the price that society pays for having designated alcohol as one of the drugs that is legal, popular, easily available and strongly advertised. The four leading causes of accidental deaths in the United States are motor vehicle crashes, falls, drownings, and fires and burns. These all constitute serious public health problems and alcohol has been implicated as a factor in each of them.

MOTOR VEHICLE CRASHES

Crashes involving motor vehicles are the leading cause of death by injury in the United States. Although the incidence of a driver being intoxicated with alcohol in fatal crashes has been reduced by almost a third over the last fifteen years, alcohol-related motor vehicle accidents continue to exert a terrible toll on this country's highways. The National Highway Traffic Safety Administration (NHTSA) reported that 46,886 people in the United States died in traffic accidents in 1987 (18). Approximately one-half of these fatalities were alcohol-related and of the 40,000 or so Americans who died in traffic accidents in 1994, about 17,500 died in crashes in which alcohol was a factor. This is fewer than in past years but still a tragically high number, and far too many lives are lost or ruined as a result of driving while intoxicated with alcohol.

Safety devices, such as seat belts and airbags, and lower speed limits, appear to have contributed to the reduction in motor vehicle deaths in the U.S. to about 40,000 a year since peaking at 56,300 in 1972. Encouragingly, statistics from NHTSA have shown that alcohol is involved less often. In 1982, 30% of all drivers involved in fatal crashes were found to be intoxicated, that is, having blood alcohol concentrations of .10% or higher. By 1992, only 21.9% drivers in fatal crashes were found to be intoxicated. Similarly, in 1982 either a driver, a pedestrian or a passenger was found to have been drinking in 57% of all fatal accidents, while by 1992, the figure was down to 45%.

In spite of these encouraging statistics, traffic accidents remain the greatest single cause of death in the United States for people between ages five and thirty-four. About 40% of all teenage deaths (15 to 19 years) occur in traffic accidents, but the number of fatal crashes involving drunk drivers has also steadily decreased. However, the total number of fatal crashes for this age group has increased, indicating that although more young drivers are becoming involved in fatal crashes, fewer of them are intoxicated at the time of the crash. Twenty-one states have now dropped the permissible alcohol level for teenage drivers to a level well below that permitted in adults. In most cases, the level for teenage drivers has been set at only .02%. Surveys suggest that many people under twenty-one who do drink are now choosing designated drivers.

There are already more than 1,200 drunken driving laws on the books in the United States, a few federal laws, and most legislatures are seriously considering having still more. Forty-four states now have laws that mandate prison time for any driver convicted twice for driving while intoxicated, and some politicians are asking for imprisonment for first-time convictions. Twelve of the states have lowered the permissible blood alcohol concentration from .10% to .08% and at least a dozen others are studying similar reductions.

Factors felt to be important in influencing the progress being made against drunk drivers include advertisements in the media that promote responsible drinking behavior and not drinking when driving, the use of designated drivers, tougher laws, and the development of organizations, such as Mothers and Students Against Drunk Driving. As a result, fewer drivers drink, and generally people who do drink tend to drink less alcohol. Bartenders are refusing more often to serve intoxicated individuals, police are increasingly vigilant and are equipped with more sophisticated instruments to measure breath alcohol. An important legal development is the administrative license revocation (ALR), which has been adopted by at least 36 states. This calls for automatic confiscation of the driver's license, and in some cases the car of any driver who refuses to take or fails a sobriety test.

Although there have been objections to ALR based on legal due process, higher courts have usually refused to overturn earlier laws. Usually, the driver is given a temporary license for a few weeks, during which time an appeal can be lodged. Knowing for certain that driving while intoxicated in an ALR state will result in immediate loss of the license appears to have an extremely significant impact.

Despite all these commendable efforts, however, an alcohol-related highway fatality still occurs every 30 minutes and the two groups most resistant to change are males between the ages of 21 and 35 years, and alcohol-dependent individuals or alcoholics who continue to drive while intoxicated whether they have a license or not.

The incidence and severity of alcohol use and abuse in persons arrested for driving while intoxicated (DWI) were investigated by Fine, et. al. (19) in 1,500 subjects arrested for DWI for the first time in the city of Philadelphia. They all had blood alcohol levels of .10% or higher, thus meeting the legal definition of intoxication in the Commonwealth of Pennsylvania.

The comprehensive interview included eleven questions designed to measure the number and degree of physical and behavioral symptoms of excessive alcohol use, and six questions designed to measure the weight and total consumption of alcoholic beverages in preceding months. The resulting alcohol impairment index is synthesized into a single number, the quantity and different types of alcoholic beverages (beer, wine, and liquor) and the frequency of intake. The rationale behind the indicator is that particular threshold values of absolute alcohol intake into the bloodstream result in varying degrees of impairment. This investigation described three general levels of alcohol impairment, which were designated as Groups 1, 2, and 3.

GROUP 1

Persons in Group 1 typically consume alcoholic beverages up to a limit of once or twice a week, depending upon the social situation. When these persons drink, they usually imbibe less than 3 quarts of beer, or less than 6 shots of whiskey, or less than 3 water glasses filled with wine. At times they may use whiskey and beer simultaneously in lesser amounts (for example, 1 quart of beer and 2 shots of whiskey). These drinkers enjoy drinking with others in social situations and rarely drink alone, although there are some exceptions. Another characteristic of drinkers in this group is that they may drink to excess once or twice a month.

GROUP 2

Group 2 is comprised of persons who drink alcohol at least twice weekly and consume during a drinking session a minimum of 5 quarts of beer, or one-fifth of wine, or 2 pints of liquor. Again, the alcohol may be consumed in different combinations (for example, 1 quart of beer, 2 glasses of wine, or 5 shots of whiskey). Group 2 drinkers exhibit one or more of the following behavioral characteristics; being "high" up to 10 times a month, a long period of continued drinking ranging over 6 hours, drinking occasionally upon awaking, reported memory lapses or "blackouts," frequent complaints of other "nervous" disorders, missing meals because of drinking habits, drinking occasionally during working hours, and possibly having an arrest for an alcohol-related incident not involving driving.

GROUP 3

People in group 3 typically consume alcoholic beverages daily, and their daily intake of alcohol is at least 5 or more quarts of beer, or one-fifth of wine, or 3 pints of whiskey. These beverages may be consumed in any combination (that is, 3 quarts of beer, 2 glasses of wine, and 2 pints of liquor). These drinkers have one or more of the following behavioral characteristics; being "high" more than 10 times a month, often drinking continuously for more than 12 hours at one drinking session, reporting memory impairments or "blackouts" for many of their drinking episodes, having their drinking habits interfere many times with their eating patterns, frequently missing a number of meals, and finally, admitting to tremor, agitation, confusion, excessive perspiration, or delirium tremens on discontinuing the use of alcohol. These persons invariably report that they begin their day with a drink and continue to drink at frequent intervals during the day. Their drinking is associated with quarrels in the family, poor work relationships, and arrests for such incidents as fighting, disturbing the peace, or public intoxication.

When categorized by the level of alcohol impairment, the sample of these fifteen-hundred offenders was found to fall into the following groups:

Impairment Group	Number of Offenders	Percent
1	685	45.7
2	721	48.1
3	94	6.3

Impairment: The data clearly demonstrate that a substantial proportion of this population (Groups 2 and 3) reported a constant, regular abuse of alcohol. Since all clients were referred from the court system, one could reasonably suspect some underreporting of alcohol intake and that the clients' anticipated fear of judicial reaction to their reported condition would cause them to minimize the reported effect of alcohol on their behavior.

Age: As shown in Table 3, there were marked differences in the level of alcohol impairment, dependent on age.

Persons under 40 years of age were more alcohol-impaired than those over 40. The statistical probability that such a disproportionate number of clients under 40 would be more abusive drinkers than those over 40 due to chance alone is less than 1 in 1,000.

This study found that 54.4% of these first offenders arrested for driving while intoxicated reported levels of alcohol impairment consistent with inclusion in Groups 2 and 3 as compared to only an expected 12% in the general population. It was evident therefore, that this study population had a quite different and more serious pattern of alcohol use than found in the population at large. A significant percentage of these individuals had drinking patterns that included an impulsive need to drink and also possibly incorporated some degree of self-destructive behavior. Although they admitted to many pathological drinking behaviors, they were poorly motivated to seek treatment and less than 2% of them reported ever having been in any treatment program related to drinking. More than 90% did not consider their drinking behavior to be a problem before their arrest.

Table 3. Impairment and Age

Impairment Group	18 to 40 years		41 years and older	
	Number	Percent	Number	Percent
1	332	40	353	52
2	434	52	287	43
3	62	8	32	5
	828	100	672	100

It is of more than academic interest to consider the impact of extremely strong sanctions against drinking and driving. Several European countries, especially Great Britain and Scandinavia, introduced such sanctions more than twenty years ago, lowering the legal blood alcohol level to .05% and making loss of the driving license and imprisonment mandatory for anyone convicted of drunken driving. Although there was an initial reduction in alcohol-related accidents, the rates of such accidents have gradually begun to rise again. Alcohol is still found to be a significant factor in the serious overall problem of motor vehicle accidents in these countries.

Another finding, which emanated from the Philadelphia DWI project, was the relationship between blood alcohol concentration and self-reported drinking behavior. The Criteria Committee of the National Council on Alcoholism (20) refers to blood alcohol concentrations as having significant value in contributing to a diagnosis. The Committee considers a BAC of .15% or more in the absence of gross evidence of intoxication to be a major criterion, "definitely" indicative of tolerance to alcohol and therefore, alcoholism. In the Committee's list of minor criteria, a BAC of .3% or more at any time or a level of more than .1% in a routine examination is also considered to be "classical, definite, obligatory," a criterion "clearly associated with alcoholism." Unfortunately, the report by this Criteria Committee included no reference to any work that had attempted to validate the assumption that these BACs are associated with other indicators of alcoholism. This is surprising when one considers that a BAC is easily and accurately obtained and, if a BAC is a positive indicator of alcoholism, it may be one of the few objective measures of the disorder.

In one particular investigation, Fine et al. (21) used a sample of 3,837 men drawn from persons who had been arrested for Driving While Intoxicated (DWI) and were being evaluated prior to attending a series of classes on safe driving, or being referred to appropriate alcoholism treatment programs. All the men had BACs of .10% or above at the time of arrest. The mean age of the men was 40.10 ± 12.43 years, the racial composition was 62% black and 38% white; 27.1% had never married, 47.0% were currently married, and the remaining 25.9% were divorced, separated or widowed. More than half had served in the armed forces, and more than a quarter (28.1%) had been arrested previously for DWI. The men reported that they had not changed their current drinking patterns for an average of 9.43 ± 10.10 years. Only 3.9% of the men had received any kind of treatment for alcohol-related problems.

The BAC scores were recorded by the Philadelphia Police Department using a Smith & Wesson Breathalyzer, Model 900. The average length of time between arrest and breath testing was 137.5 ± 74.1 minutes. Two indices of alcohol use and impairment were employed. Both indices were developed by the Stanford Research Institute For The Treatment Center Monitoring System of the National Institute on Alcohol Abuse and Alcoholism (22). The measure of alcohol consumption was a Quantity-Frequency (Q-F) index, the sum of the frequencies with which beer, wine and distilled spirits were drunk during a typical day during the past month, multiplied by the absolute alcohol content of each beverage. The Q-F scores could range from 0 to 106.7 oz.

The measure of behavioral impairment related to excessive use of alcohol, also developed by the Stanford Research Institute, was the Impairment Index (23). The Index consists of twelve questions about the extent of self-perceived problems attributed to excessive use of alcohol during the past month. The items are rated on either 2 or 3-point scales, and a total score, ranging from 0 to 32 is derived by summing the 12 ratings. The internal consistency of this Index is .90.

As expected from associated research in this study, the distribution of the Q-F and impairment indices were positively skewed, suggesting strongly that the men were denying the extent of their alcohol use and the symptoms related to excessive alcohol use. The mean Q-F score was 1.4 ± 2.0, and the mean score on the Impairment Index was 5.3 ± 3.98. The mean Breathalyzer score obtained at the time of arrest was $0.19 \pm .05\%$. The distribution of the Breathalyzer scores was rectangular, indicating that the scores were equally represented throughout their range of .10 to .40%.

The results suggest that the BAC levels were related to other indices of alcohol impairment in this sample of drunken drivers, a group which has been shown to minimize their own drinking and alcohol-related behavior. Since these relationships are present in this population, it may be postulated that even firmer relationships would exist in patients, who as a group would be probably be more honest in their reporting because they are not subject to judicial scrutiny. The measurements of patients' BACs could therefore be valuable indicators of alcohol-related syndromes.

The fact that Breathalyzer scores are associated with the reported quantity and frequency of alcohol consumed as well as with a variety of other behavioral characteristics of alcoholics, makes the BAC a valuable and objective criterion for the diagnosis of alcoholism. Access to patients' BACs could aid physicians considerably in their evaluation of patients suspected of misusing alcohol, and this is especially so in the evaluations of offenders arrested for DWI.

Because of the complex legal, social, psychological, and medical ramifications involved, driving while intoxicated is a social problem that requires integration of the criminal justice system with the mental health system for its efficient management. Although the criminal justice system should continue to have the primary responsibility for managing drunk drivers, that system acting alone will inevitably find it cannot effect the behavioral changes that must occur for the problem to be significantly reduced. Any management system must include those treatment stratagems within the mental health system that are directed specifically toward that kind of pathological dependency on alcohol, which has been demonstrated in such a large proportion of these offenders.

AIRCRAFT CRASHES

The role of alcohol in aircraft crashes appears to be relatively insignificant. Wolk (24) states that less than 2% of commercial aircraft crashes are associated with alcohol intoxication, but typical estimates of alcohol involvement by pilots in general aviation crashes range from 10% to 30%. Fortunately, pilots, by and large, tend to be extremely responsible individuals who are knowledgeable of and respect the fact that alcohol can seriously impair pilot performance.

There are also strict regulations regarding the use of alcohol or drugs by pilots and other crew members of aircraft. These are as follows:

A) No person may act or attempt to act as a crew member of a civil aircraft:

1) Within 8 hours after the consumption of any alcoholic beverage;

2) While under the influence of alcohol;

3) While using any drug that affects the person's faculties in any way contrary to safety; or

4) While having .04% by weight or more alcohol in the blood.

B) Except in an emergency, no pilot of a civil aircraft may allow a person who appears to be intoxicated or who demonstrates by manner or physical indications that the individual is under the influence of drugs (except a medical patient under proper care) to be carried in that aircraft.

C) A crew member shall do the following:

1) On request of a law enforcement officer, submit to a test to indicate the percentage by weight of alcohol in the blood when

i) The law enforcement officer is authorized under state or local law to conduct the test or to have the test conducted; and

ii) The law enforcement officer is requesting submission to the test to investigate a suspected violation of state or local law governing the same or substantially similar conduct prohibited by paragraph (A) (1), (A) (2), or (a) (4) of this section.

2) Whenever the Administrator has a reasonable basis to believe that a person may have violated paragraph (A) (1), (A) (4) of this section, that person shall, upon request by the Administrator, furnish the Administrator or authorize any clinic, hospital, doctor or other person to release to the Administrator, the results of each test taken within 4 hours after acting or attempting to act as a crew member that indicates percentage by weight of alcohol in the blood.

D) Whenever the Administrator has a reasonable basis to believe that a person may have violated paragraph (A) (3) of this section, that person shall, upon request by the Administrator, furnish the Administrator or authorize any clinic, hospital, doctor, or other person to release to the Administrator, the results of each test taken within 4 hours after acting or attempting to act as a crew member that indicates the presence of any drugs in the body.

E) Any test information obtained by the Administrator under paragraph (c) or (d) of this section may be evaluated in determining a person's qualifications for any airman certificate or possible violations of this chapter and may be used as evidence in any legal proceeding under section 602, 609, or 901 of the Federal Aviation Act of 1958.

Fortunately, these regulations are strictly adhered to, and we do not, therefore, have the same concerns about traveling our skies as we do about traveling on our highways.

BOATING ACCIDENTS

In stark contrast to aircraft pilots, 35% of boat owners admitted to drinking alcohol while operating their boats. A Coast Guard survey (25) found that of 16 million boaters interviewed, 40% reported carrying alcohol on board while underway. It is not surprising, therefore, that a significant proportion of boating accidents are associated with alcohol intoxication. Also, alcohol was "possibly" involved in 60% of boating fatalities (including persons who fell overboard).

In their review of the literature from 1950 to 1985, Hingson and Howland found that from 17% to 31% of boaters who drowned had consumed alcohol (26). However, since the consumption of alcohol by boaters in general is possibly more than that consumed by boaters who drown, any causal relationship between alcohol and drowning in boating accidents appears to be a rather weak one.

The third leading cause of accidental death in the United States is drowning, but the available data are not sufficient to establish a causal role for alcohol in drowning. Intoxication with alcohol would certainly increase the likelihood of an individual drowning because of lack of judgment, increased bravado and impulsivity. Also, alcohol can result in disorientation, impairment of psychomotor skills, reduced ability for breathholding and pathological thermal response to water temperature.

There seems little doubt that if alcohol ceased to be a so-called recreational drug of choice for boaters, swimmers and those engaged in other water sports, there would be an appreciable reduction in morbidity and mortality. As the number of high-powered speedboats and jet skis, often operated by inexperienced teenagers and young adults, increases, the role of alcohol in accidents involving these crafts will become of increasing concern and stricter legislation and enforcement will be needed.

FALLING ACCIDENTS

The second leading cause of fatal accidents in the United States is falls of various kinds. Approximately 13,000 deaths annually are the result of falls and, as would be expected, alcohol intoxication significantly increases the risk for such falls. In their study of alcohol as a risk factor for injury or death resulting from accidental falls, Hingson and Howland (27) found that the percentage of alcohol-related falls resulting in fatalities ranged between 17% and 53%, and for non-fatal falls, between 21% and 77%.

The role of alcohol in accidental falls has been studied by Honkanen et al. (28) who found that 60% of emergency room patients who had fallen had measurable blood alcohol concentrations (BACs) and 53% had BACs above .20%. They showed also that compared with control subjects, the risk of falling increased with the blood alcohol concentration. Those with BACs of .05% to .10% were three times more likely to fall than individuals with no alcohol. BACs of .10% to 15% carried ten times the risk, and those with BACs of .16% or higher were sixty times more likely to fall.

Individuals who slip and fall are often the subject of litigation, and many of these cases are associated with alcohol intoxication. The role that alcohol might have played in such accidents often determines liability, and experts asked to testify in such cases should have expertise in understanding and explaining the pharmacology of alcohol, the importance of blood alcohol concentrations, and the behaviors expected at such concentrations.

ACCIDENTS INVOLVING FIRES AND BURNS

The fourth leading cause of accidental deaths from injuries in the United States, resulting in approximately six thousand fatalities a year, is from burn injuries. Thirty-two studies that were published between 1947 and 1986 dealing with alcohol and injuries from fires and burns were analyzed by Howland and Hingson (29), and many of these investigations point to an association between alcohol consumption and an increased risk of fires and burns.

In Toronto, a study dealing with alcoholics in treatment between 1961 and 1963 found that the death rate by fire was 9.7 times the rate expected on the basis of mortality statistics in Ontario (30).

Also, another study demonstrated that treated alcoholics in St. Louis had twenty-six times the number of deaths by fire as to be expected from St. Louis mortality statistics (31). One study in California indicated that 64% of individuals whose deaths were caused by fire had BACs of .10% or higher at the time of their deaths (32). This compared with 18% of individuals who died after episodes of a chief illness whose BAC s were .10% or above at the time of death.

There is little doubt that alcohol consumption represents an appreciable risk factor for deaths by fire, and several studies have also indicated that the use of alcohol is more frequent among victims of fires caused by cigarettes (33). Approximately one-third of all fire fatalities occur in house fires caused by cigarettes, so that alcohol used in conjunction with cigarette smoking produces a very serious risk for fires and injuries resulting from them.

6

ALCOHOL AND CRIMINAL RESPONSIBILITY

Intoxication with alcohol is of particular interest to forensic psychiatry, not only because it is so common, but also because it demands consideration of most legal issues concerned in the determination of criminal responsibility. The legal issues that surround intoxication with alcohol or other drugs and the intent to commit an offense are extremely complicated and, as stated very succinctly by Smith:

"A scholar in search of logic, consistency and clarity of expression in the law would do well to look elsewhere than in the cases involving intoxication as a defense" (34).

Voluntary intoxication has always been regarded by the law as more of an aggravating factor, and as long ago as the 4th Century B.C., Aristotle had this to say about intoxication and alcohol:

"Indeed we punish a man for his very ignorance, if he is thought responsible for the ignorance, as when penalties are doubled in the case of drunkenness; for the moving principle is in the man himself, since he had the power of not getting drunk and his getting drunk was the cause of his ignorance. And we punish those who are ignorant of anything in the laws that they ought to know and that is not difficult, and so too in the case of anything else they are thought to be ignorant, since they have the power of taking care" (35).

As d'Orban (36) has indicated, by the 4th Century B.C., "we already find the doctrine clearly expressed that even if the drunken man did not know what he was doing, he is guilty because of his recklessness in getting himself into that state."

When considering a defense of a criminal charge where alcohol is a factor, there are really only two circumstances where alcohol or drug use are relevant:

1) When intoxication causes the accused to not be able to find the intent necessary to commit the offense.

2) If the alcohol or drugs are causative in the production of psychiatric illness.

The forensic psychiatrist would do well to remember that the ultimate purpose of providing expert evidence is to present the court with truly scientific information, which is not likely to be familiar to jurors or judges. Forensic psychiatrists have no special expertise in areas that are considered to be matters of common knowledge or experience, and psychiatric testimony should only be considered when there is diagnosable psychiatric illness in the defendant. Acceptance of the limitation of their expertise would lead to increased credibility and acceptance of psychiatric testimony, and forensic psychiatrists should be extremely open and honest in accepting these realistic proscriptions on what they can and cannot provide to the court.

A positive correlation between alcohol use and criminal activity has been highlighted for many years, but it is important to note that a direct cause and effect relationship between these two variables has not yet been fully established. There is no question that prisoners in jails report a high incidence of alcohol problems, and alcohol abusers engage more often in criminal behavior than do people who either do not drink alcohol or are so-called social drinkers.

Most of the serious crime in the United States is committed by late adolescents or young adults, and drinking alcohol also becomes a problem during adolescence and increases in severity during the late teens and early twenties. This population of young people is inexperienced in drinking alcohol and tends to be more immature and poorly controlled. It might well be that any causal relationship between alcohol and crime is therefore related primarily to the age of the perpetrator.

Spousal abuse is a phenomenon that is receiving increasing publicity and attention, and many abused wives report that their husbands are alcohol abusers or alcohol-dependent people. Husbands who abuse their wives also report a relationship between the abuse and their use of alcohol. Physically abusive men have been found to have significantly higher scores on a screening test for alcoholism than men in two comparison groups (37). Clinically, it is evident that physical violence by men towards their spouses is much more common in those designated as alcohol dependent, and these individuals often have coincident recurrent depression and, or, an anti-social personality disorder. Some families seem to be characterized by physical violence and other negative interactions occurring in the context of alcohol use and abuse.

Several studies (38) and clinical experience strongly suggest that there is also an association between alcohol problems and child abuse. A study by Bland and Orn (39), suggested that parents who abuse their children were also more likely to report physical violence towards their spouses, as well as involvement in other fights with adults and fights involving weapons.

For many years it has been well recognized by investigators that alcohol is involved in 50-60% of homicides, and often both the killer and the victim have been under the influence of alcohol at the time of the crime. When the forensic psychiatrist is asked to provide expert evidence in the courtroom, and where alcohol is a factor, the relationship between intoxication and impairment, and the accepted status of drug and alcohol dependence as a type of mental illness, can present very specific problems. Also, in such cases, the general problems with regards to any kind of expert testimony are important issues that have to be taken into consideration.

With regard to the specific problems associated with the use of alcohol, the task of the forensic psychiatrist is to elicit whether the alcohol use has resulted in the production of a mental disorder, or if the degree of intoxication resulted in the accused being unable to form the necessary intent to commit the offense. If the offense was committed in the context of a psychosis induced by alcohol, or during delirium tremens, a plea of not guilty by reason of insanity might be considered. Although the alcohol-induced psychosis might be temporary and relatively short-lived, a case can still be made that the individual was suffering from insanity at the time of the crime.

In Great Britain, the defense of insanity is now very rarely raised, and it has been replaced by a defense of "diminished responsibility," even in cases of murder. In the United States, being intoxicated with alcohol at the time of the murder, might help to reduce the charge from a first degree homicide to a lesser degree.

Although voluntary intoxication is no defense to a criminal charge, there have been efforts to introduce litigating elements into the law so that the intoxicated individual would be viewed differently from the sober offender in the case of serious crimes.

Such changes began in the 19th century in Great Britain, when penalties of death or transportation were applied for serious crimes, and measures were introduced in an attempt to exonerate the intoxicated offender from a serious offense and allow the court to convict for a less serious charge that did not carry such a severe penalty. As a result, the term "specific intent" was applied to those crimes involving an intention going beyond the *actus reus* (the prohibited deed), whereas crimes where the intent was limited to the act which actually constitutes the crime, were said to require only "basic intent."

Examples of crimes requiring specific intent would be burglary, fraud, wounding with intent to cause grievous bodily harm and murder, while offenses such as assault or manslaughter would be regarded as requiring just basic intent. Unfortunately, this distinction did not lend itself to definitional clarity, so that the decision as to whether a crime is one of specific or basic intent has generally been decided by case law. Intoxication, with alcohol or other drugs, may be introduced as a defense to those crimes requiring specific intent if the accused person was shown to be intoxicated to such a degree that the specific intent required in the definition of the offense could not have been formed.

In 1920, an intoxication defense was introduced in the case of a man who had suffocated a girl while raping her, and a brilliant commentary on this type of defense was made at the time by Lord Birkenhead (40). With some modifications, this is applicable even today:

"where a specific intent is an essential element in the offense, evidence of a state of drunkenness rendering the accused incapable of forming such an intent should be taken into consideration in order to determine whether he had in fact formed the intent necessary to constitute the particular crime. If he was so drunk that he was incapable of forming the intent required, he could not be convicted of a crime which was committed only if the intent was proved. In a charge of murder based upon intention to kill or to do grievous bodily harm, if the jury are satisfied that the accused was, by reason of his drunken condition, incapable of forming the intent to kill or to do grievous bodily harm...he cannot be convicted of murder. But nevertheless, unlawful homicide has been committed by the accused... and that is beyond manslaughter... .The law is plain beyond all question that in cases falling short of insanity a condition of drunkenness at the time of committing an offense causing death can only, when it is available at all, have the effect of reducing the crime from murder to manslaughter."

Since this formulation, the emphasis has changed from the offender's capacity to form intent to whether or not he did in fact form the intent to commit the crime. Consideration has also been given to the situation where defendants deliberately drink to a state of intoxication in order to give them "courage" to commit their crime. In such cases, one cannot escape conviction on the grounds that this voluntary intoxication led to the inability to form the necessary intent.

7

THE DRAM SHOP ACT

Legal sanctions around the use of alcohol developed in 1607 when alcoholic beverages were brought to America with the settling of the Virginia Colony. By 1619, the excessive use of alcohol resulted in a law decreeing that any person found drunk for the first time was to be reproved privately by the minister; the second time publicly; the third time to "lye in halter" for twelve hours and pay a fine. Various efforts to control drinking and drunkenness are therefore not modern phenomena, but have been with us for an exceedingly long time. Under common law, courts did not recognize any cause of action against anyone who furnished alcohol. This refusal to recognize any cause of action against one who furnished or provided alcohol became known as the "Consumption Rule."

By the middle of the 19th century, various state legislatures passed "dram shop" or "civil action" statutes which placed civil liability upon tavern keepers, saloon keepers and other purveyors of intoxicating liquors for injuries caused by service of intoxicants to minors or visibly intoxicated patrons. In the Commonwealth of Pennsylvania, the first such act was the Dram Shop Act of May 8, 1854 (41), which provided in pertinent part:

"[Section 3.] That any person furnishing intoxicating drinks to another person in violation of any existing law, or the provisions of these acts, (sic) shall be held civilly responsible for any injury to person or property in consequence of such furnishing, and any one aggrieved may recover full damages against such persons so furnishing by action on the case, instituted in any court having jurisdiction of such a form of action in this Commonwealth."

This act, as amended over the years, and in conjunction with the criminal statutes proscribing sales of intoxicating liquors to minors and individuals who were visibly intoxicated, was the basis for liability against licensees. Case examples are *Fink v. Carman*, (42) where an individual who was served alcohol while visibly intoxicated staggered outside of a saloon and was run over by a wagon; the saloon keeper was held liable to the widow; *Davies v. Knight* (43) where a saloon keeper found liable to a widow for the serving of intoxicating liquors to an individual who was visibly intoxicated with the result that the patron fell into a gutter of water and died as a result of "chill," and *McCusker v. Quinn* (44) in which a saloon keeper was found liable to the survivors of a patron who fell out of a saloon door after being sold intoxicants while visibly intoxicated.

"The Dram Shop" act was repealed by the adoption of the Pennsylvania Liquor Code, Act of April 12, 1951 (45). Section 4-493 of the Liquor Code provides in pertinent part:

> "It shall be unlawful for any licensee or the board, or any employee, servant or agent of such licensee or the board, or any other person, to sell, furnish or give any liquor or malted or brewed beverages or to permit any liquor or brewed beverages to be sold, furnished or given, to any person visibly intoxicated, or to any insane person, or to any minor, or to habitual drunkards, or persons of known intempered habits."

Section 47 P.S. 4-497 provides as follows:

> "No licensee shall be liable to third persons on account of damages inflicted upon them off the licensed premises by customers of the licensee unless the customer who inflicts the damages was sold, furnished or given liquor or malted or brewed beverages by the said licensee or his agent, servant or employee when said customer was visibly intoxicated."

Section 497 was added in 1964 by the legislature in response to language of justice (later Chief Justice) Eagan in the case of *Smith v. Clark* (46). In that case, Justice Eagan wrote:

"the serving of intoxicants to minors or to visibly intoxicated persons are separate and distinct violations, there can be no doubt."

Under the liquor code, liability is imposed upon a licensee for service of intoxicating liquors to a visibly intoxicated individual or a minor, *inter alia,* if the plaintiff shows the service of the intoxicants and that the furnishing of intoxicants was a substantial factor, that is, proximate cause of the injuries sustained by the plaintiff.

Liquor liability cases can be extremely complicated and it is essential to obtain an accurate, comprehensive account of events as detailed in depositions, hospital records and police reports, etc. A report provided by an expert to an attorney should include a detailed chronology of the relevant times, occurrences, and conduct of the alleged intoxicated patron (AIP) for the hours prior to and after his/her arrival at the drinking establishment. Facts that must be included are whether food was consumed prior to or during their drinking, a very detailed and accurate account of the type and amount of alcohol consumed before reaching the bar, during the time there, and after leaving, to the time of the incident in question.

The events that result in a case being brought before the courts include motor vehicle accidents, serious injuries or deaths following fights, accidents, such as serious falls, drownings or electrocutions, rape, murder or suicide. Where harm has resulted to the intoxicated individual, restaurants, bars or even private homes can, and have been, held liable for both compensatory and punitive damages that are often enormous.

The expert must obtain a most detailed account of the incident in question with particular emphasis on the role of the alleged intoxicated individual. This information is often contained in police reports as well as depositions.

The most important part of the history is the behavior of the individual or individuals in question while they were present at the drinking establishment. Accurate and reliable eyewitness accounts of this behavior are critical and probably mean more to a jury than any other single fact.

It is, therefore, worthwhile for experts to emphasize to attorneys the great need for such eyewitness accounts, although many times these accounts are not available. Descriptions by reliable eyewitnesses of behavior clearly indicative of visible intoxication are difficult to refute and can be extremely damaging to the defense in these cases.

Equally, it is a great advantage to the defense to have eyewitness accounts describing the absence of intoxication, and the more often these can be corroborated, the more favorable the outcome should be for the defense. In practice, there are usually conflicting accounts of the behavior in question, and the defense in these situations will need to emphasize those behaviors that might be compatible with being in a bar setting and which do not necessarily indicate visible intoxication. For example, in an establishment where music is being played, it is not unusual for patrons to be dancing or swaying in time with the music, and even when such behavior is obvious to others, it does not necessarily imply visible intoxication. Also, laughing, joking and generally responding to the atmosphere of a "swinging" establishment does not necessarily lead to the conclusion of visible intoxication.

On the other hand, stumbling and falling while dancing, or climbing on tables or on the bar, would not be regarded as acceptable behavior in most establishments and, therefore, might be consistent with visible intoxication. Thus, it is important to remember that the conduct must be of the type which would put the bar on notice that the patron should no longer be served.

Knowledge of blood alcohol levels is always of paramount importance in these cases. The usual scenario is that some time after the alleged offense, a blood alcohol concentration is determined for one or more individuals. This is sometimes obtained from a Breathalyzer taken by the police or a direct blood or serum alcohol concentration obtained usually in a hospital. Experts are often asked to calculate or "relate back" from this known blood alcohol level, the estimated blood alcohol concentration that would have been present at the time of the offense, and also what that blood alcohol concentration would have been at the time the individual, or individuals were drinking at the restaurant or bar. It should be emphasized that the actual blood alcohol level at the time the person was consuming alcohol in the establishment is rarely, if ever, known. Estimates of the blood alcohol concentration are therefore always open to question and damaging cross-examination.

Whether the blood alcohol concentration was rising or falling is also often an issue. For example, if most of the drinking was done rapidly over a very short period of time just before leaving the drinking establishment, the blood alcohol concentration might have been relatively low in the bar with little or no evidence of visible intoxication; but as the blood alcohol level kept rising after the individual left the bar, a high reading could have been obtained later when signs of intoxication were present.

Toxicologic issues concerning blood alcohol levels include questions about the validity of the sample of blood, urine or bile, and possible contamination, the accuracy and reliability of the recording instruments, whether it is a breath, blood or serum level that is measured, and the site from which the sample of blood was taken. For example, at autopsy, blood is often taken from the chambers of the heart or from various body cavities. In these cases, the reported blood alcohol concentration is artificially high by several-fold and many times not a true representation of the blood alcohol that was circulating before death.

At first blush, it would appear that a significant blood alcohol level found in the alleged intoxicated individual would bode well for the injured party. Many jurors have been educated as to the legal blood alcohol level allowable for the purpose of operating a motor vehicle (usually .10%, but this figure varies from state to state). However, a great many cases litigated to a verdict in Pennsylvania have resulted in a favorable outcome to the liquor licensee even where the blood alcohol concentration ranges from .25% to .40%. Where a high blood alcohol concentration has been shown to be present, the best defense strategy would appear to be the demonstration of tolerance to alcohol (or cross-tolerance with other drugs), and eyewitnesses who can testify to the absence of signs of visible intoxication.

It is essential that a careful history of the past drinking behavior of the individual be obtained both from the subject and, if possible, from relatives and friends. Also, access to medical records which include social histories that might indicate that problem drinking or alcoholism was present is extremely useful. The quantity and frequency of alcohol usually consumed, the number of years of use, and reports of how the individual appeared when drinking in the past are all important.

One of the consequences of drinking large amounts of alcohol over long periods of time is change in sensitivity of the brain to the effects of alcohol. This results in larger quantities of alcohol being required to produce the same effects. Tolerance is the name given to this adaptation and its most dramatic manifestations are seen in alcohol-dependent persons. These individuals have to consume extremely large quantities of alcohol to produce the changes in behavior and feelings that were previously attained with much smaller quantities of alcohol. Also, they are able to drink these large amounts without conspicuously losing control of their senses or ability to ambulate and function. The alcoholic individual may drink a fifth of whiskey or more a day without showing signs of drunkenness. Complex tasks can be performed accurately by such individuals with blood alcohol levels several times as great as those that would incapacitate infrequent drinkers. Tolerance can be innate, determined by genetic influences, or acquired through many years of exposure to large doses of alcohol.

It is this phenomenon of tolerance that allows the liquor licensee to argue that signs that are usually present at certain blood alcohol levels do not necessarily occur to the same degree in persons who can be established as having developed tolerance to alcohol. Thus, reports that state categorically that signs, such as boisterousness, staggering gait, spilling drinks or dropping glasses, or even stumbling and falling, will inevitably be present at a blood alcohol of, for example, .15%, can be justifiably criticized when tolerance has not been taken into consideration. Where there is a definitive history of alcohol dependence, it is possible to claim convincingly that high blood levels are not necessarily accompanied by signs of visible intoxication. It must be noted that many toxicologists who are involved with the testing and observation of the conduct of intoxicated individuals are unwilling to accept the phenomenon of tolerance. They are thus "sitting ducks" for vigorous cross-examination of something most jurors see on a daily basis.

In those jurisdictions which allow for a cause of action by the alleged intoxicated patron (AIP) against the licensee, juries have been overwhelmingly responsive to a defense position premised upon the negligence or responsibility of the injured party. Counsel may thus argue that the injured party was solely responsible for damages both as to the ingestion of alcohol (no one forced it down his or her throat) and conduct as an intoxicated driver, pedestrian or passenger. Juries for the most part have little patience for the adult drunk who injures himself, and even in the face of evidence of visible intoxication, decide that the bar is not negligent.

While the standard remains the same (service of a patron while visibly intoxicated), the more difficult case to defend involves the injuring or killing of an innocent victim by the AIP. Defense counsel must first overcome the natural anger and sympathy the jury feels for the victim or his or her family in addition to the bias many jurors subscribe to in dealing with providers of alcohol. In many cases, this anger results in a verdict of countless millions in both compensatory and punitive damages.

An example of an interesting Dram Shop Act Case is that litigated in the Commonwealth of Pennsylvania (*Estate of v. Dino's Lounge, et al.*) (47).

At about 1:45 A.M. on April 16, 1983, the decedent, Edwin Boudwin left the Wild Irishman Tavern. It was dark and raining heavily as he ran across an abutting highway and was struck by an automobile driven by Robert Hochstuhl. Mr. Hochstuhl pulled over, left his vehicle and upon investigating the incident was unable to find anything other than a sneaker and a segment of an exterior rear view mirror. The police were notified and on arrival, were able to find nothing more. However, a short time later, and approximately eight-tenths of a mile from the Wild Irishman, another motorist, James Neff, ran over an object lying in the westbound lane. Although at the time of impact, Mr. Neff did not realize that the object was a human being, it was later determined to be the body of Edwin Boudwin.

No evidence had been uncovered which would enable one to establish how the body of Edwin Boudwin came to the place where Mr. Neff's car struck it. There was some speculation that the body became attached to a third unknown vehicle and was dragged to the point where Mr. Neff ran over it.

Allen Prindle, who was a friend of the decedent, had met Boudwin on the evening of April 15, 1983 at approximately 5:00 P.M. in a bar known as Paul's Tavern in Delaware County, Pennsylvania. Edwin Boudwin had been seated at the bar with a drink in front of him and the two remained at Paul's Tavern for approximately two hours, during which time Mr. Boudwin was observed to consume three more drinks. At approximately 7:00 P.M., Allen Prindle left the Tavern, went home and returned at approximately 8:00 P.M. when he again saw Edwin Boudwin. Before the two left Paul's Tavern, Edward Boudwin was seen to have ingested two more drinks. Prindle and Boudwin then left Paul's Tavern and went to Dino's Lounge located four or five miles away. They remained at Dino's from approximately 10:15 P.M. until 1:00 AM. of the fateful morning, during which period Mr. Prindle said the decedent consumed three more drinks. Allen Prindle then drove Edwin Boudwin to the Wild Irishman Tavern located a short distance away and Mr. Boudwin went inside while Mr. Prindle returned to Dino's Lounge. A short time later, at 1:45 A.M., the decedent left the Wild Irishman Tavern and was killed as a pedestrian crossing the highway in front of the Wild Irishman Tavern.

The plaintiff, Patricia Boudwin, brought this action as the wife of the decedent and administrator of his estate and guardian of their daughter. The plaintiff sued the three taverns mentioned above, along with the two drivers, Robert Hochstuhl and James Neff. Allen Prindle was joined as an additional defendant. The court, prior to trial, granted Allen Prindle's motion for summary judgment. Further, following the presentation of evidence, the case was dismissed as to defendants Neff and Wild Irishman Tavern.

As is customary in these cases, depositions were obtained from those individuals who had observed Edwin Boudwin during the nine hour period preceding his death. All those who saw him, with the exception of one individual, Susan Romano, had indicated that he showed no visible signs of intoxication and so testified at trial. Susan Romano, who had worked as a bartender at the Wild Irishman, knew Mr. Boudwin for approximately three years including one as a regular customer of the Wild Irishman.

At the time of her deposition, Romano testified as to Boudwin's conduct after she arrived at Dino's Lounge at approximately 10:30

P.M. She had worked at the Wild Irishman Tavern until 6:00 that evening but had not seen Boudwin as a customer at that establishment. She confirmed at her deposition that Boudwin appeared loud, thrust his fist in the air while a band was playing and slurred his words during the ten minutes she was in his company. More importantly, however, she confirmed that had she not known him personally, she would not have known he was intoxicated. At the trial, she disagreed with her deposition testimony as to this critical point.

A second witness for the plaintiff testified that the decedent had consumed approximately eleven drinks at Paul's and Dino's, while another bartender testified that she had served Edwin Boudwin at least five drinks. While the number of drinks, or quantity of alcohol that was actually consumed by the decedent during the nine hour period preceding his death is never specifically confirmed in the record, it was indeed clear that he did have a significant number of drinks, as his blood alcohol content was measured at .30%.

All those who saw Edwin Boudwin, with the exception of Susan Romano, stated that he showed no visible signs of intoxication. It is possible that the jury saw Susan Romano as a well-meaning friend, attempting to help, thereby not finding her credible concerning the visibility of the decedent's intoxication. In addition to being a regular customer at the Wild Irishman, Mr. Boudwin was also a regular customer at the Red Carpet Bar in Wilmington, Delaware, where Ms. Romano also had worked as a bartender. On cross-examination, Ms. Romano testified that she did not see the decedent stumble or walk with an unsteady gait, nor did she observe Mr. Boudwin spill any of his drinks, fall into other patrons or argue with anyone in the bar. She also indicated that throughout the entire course of her time with the decedent, she did not observe him to be aggressive toward anyone in the bar or become loud with anyone but her. Also, Ms. Romano did not see any drinks served to Mr. Boudwin in Dino's Lounge prior to his arrival to the Wild Irishman nor did she observe him to be rowdy or unruly.

Another witness, Donna Fries, who had also been a bartender at Paul's Tavern during April, 1983, testified that Mr. Boudwin "could hold his liquor—he was a man's man. He liked to go sit and have a couple drinks, and everything. Just bullshit. But he could drink good, you know, he would just sit there and talk to the guys and everything." Ms. Fries also admitted to having lived with Mr. Boudwin for a short period of time.

Testimony given by Allen Prindle was that during the afternoon and evening hours of April 15, 1983, the decedent consumed some eleven drinks. The plaintiff, Patricia Boudwin, testified to the jury that she believed that her husband had been an habitual drunkard.

Plaintiff presented the testimony of the coroner, Dr. Contostavlos, a pathologist, as to cause of death and Dr. Schweda, a toxicologist, as to the effect of the elevated blood alcohol level.

Defendant, Dino's Lounge, offered the expert testimony of Eric W. Fine, M.D., an expert in the field of psychiatry, with a subspecialty in drug and alcohol addiction. Dr. Fine testified that a phenomenon known as tolerance occurs where one who is a regular, or habitual drinker, can have a blood alcohol level of .30% or higher and yet show no visible signs of intoxication, by virtue of a biophysical masking process. This lent credence to the eyewitness accounts describing the absence of overt signs of intoxication on the part of Boudwin.

The jury exonerated the remaining defendant licensees, Paul's Tavern, and Dino's Lounge, as well as the striking motorist, Robert Hochstuhl, finding that, based on all of the evidence presented, there simply was not visible intoxication.

Several issues were involved in the successful litigation of this case. The testimony of the forensic toxicologist, Dr. Schweda, relied on well-founded data that show convincingly that most individuals with a blood alcohol level of .30% are in a state of visible intoxication. The position of the defendant was that, despite a blood alcohol level of .30%, no convincing evidence was presented that Edwin Boudwin was observed to be visibly intoxicated. In the earliest discussion stages involving Attorney Gemberling and Dr. Fine, it was recognized that a major hurdle to be crossed was attempting to convince the jury that even with this inordinately high level of alcohol in his blood, Boudwin was not in a state of visible intoxication. To accomplish this, it was decided that two essential issues to be presented to the jury were the phenomenon of tolerance to alcohol, and the paucity of eyewitness observations that Boudwin was at any time in a state that would be considered as visible intoxication.

So far as tolerance was concerned, it had to be shown that Boudwin was a very heavy imbiber of alcohol and that he had been exposed to alcohol for many years. It was also necessary to demonstrate to the jury that he had been observed to drink in the past in a manner consistent with his being able to consume large quantities of alcohol and show limited, if any, signs of intoxication. Mr. Gemberling and Dr. Fine decided that when taking depositions, information should be obtained about the decedent's drinking history - how long he had been consuming alcohol and in what quantity, whether or not he had been treated for alcohol dependence, and how he had been observed to behave when drinking. The search for this specific kind of information resulted in one witness, Donna Fries, testifying very convincingly that Mr. Boudwin was able to "hold his liquor" and was able to behave quite appropriately and involve himself in discussion with friends after consuming a significant quantity of alcohol. Also, his wife, Patricia Boudwin, told the jury that her husband had been a "habitual drunkard."

Another fact which helped to convince the jury that Boudwin was a regular consumer of alcohol and certainly not a neophyte drinker or a light social drinker, was that the autopsy report noted that he had fatty degeneration of the liver. When this was noted by Dr. Fine, he and Mr. Gemberling were able to develop a theme that Mr. Boudwin had been such a heavy consumer of alcohol during his life that he had developed fatty degeneration of his liver and that this was often an early developmental stage leading to cirrhosis of the liver. It could then be explained to the jury that not only were his drinking history and observation of his drinking behavior significant, but also objective pathological evidence existed to show that he had been a very heavy and chronic abuser of alcohol to an extent that he could very easily have been diagnosed as having alcohol dependence. The argument could then be forcefully made that he did indeed have significant tolerance to alcohol as this is known definitively to occur in chronic alcoholic patients.

The way in which this information is presented to the jury is of critical importance. The jurors have to be convinced that the expert witness has had extensive experience in observing individuals with a wide range of known blood alcohol levels. Convincing the jurors that the phenomenon of tolerance does indeed occur, and is of great significance in determining what particular behavior is seen at particular blood alcohol levels, is essential. Most jurors have had experience of drinking alcohol themselves and recognize the fact that some individuals are able to drink very large quantities of alcohol compared with others and yet show no signs of visible intoxication. Most of us know people who, even when they begin to drink, have a greater propensity for "holding their liquor" than others. This helps to demonstrate that in some individuals hereditary factors play a part in determining tolerance to alcohol, while in others the phenomenon is acquired after many years of exposure to large quantities of alcohol.

In many cases, both hereditary and acquired factors determine the level of tolerance. The ultimate message to get across was that Boudwin would have been perfectly capable of reaching a blood alcohol level of .30% and yet show no visible signs of intoxication.

Another issue that needs to be demonstrated to the jury is that the blood alcohol level in a particular individual quite clearly indicates impairment in driving ability but does not necessarily indicate overt or visible intoxication. It is accurate and honest to tell the jury that, for example, at .10% a person is unfit to safely operate an automobile but does not necessarily exhibit the signs and symptoms of visible intoxication. Equally, it was obviously conceded that at .30%, Boudwin would have been quite incapable of driving his car safely but this did not imply necessarily that he was visibly intoxicated. Questions about this are often raised by plaintiff's attorneys and the difference between being impaired as a result of alcohol as compared with visible intoxication needs to be emphasized.

In addition to the phenomenon of tolerance to alcohol is the equally important issue of eyewitness observation of Mr. Boudwin during the time he was drinking prior to his demise.

As has been emphasized, only one witness suggested in any way that he showed signs of visible intoxication, and even these observations were open to question. The fact that several witnesses observed no signs of visible intoxication was extremely convincing to the jury. In this area also it is important to educate the jury about the signs of visible intoxication. Questioning witnesses about the presence of specific signs, such as slurring of speech, spilling of drinks, excessively boisterous behavior, as well as stumbling or falling, gives the jurors a picture of what the defendant manifested while drinking. If no such behaviors were observed, it is hard to convince the jury that a bartender should have made a judgment that the defendant was visibly intoxicated. Also, there is a behavior pattern in a bar or restaurant where drinks are being consumed that can be regarded as normal. Bars are places where there is often a good deal of camaraderie with speech being louder than usual and laughter and joking not being inappropriate. Therefore, the fact that a defendant was observed to be behaving in a way that was shared by many others at the bar would not entitle a bartender to necessarily consider him to be visibly intoxicated and refuse to serve further drinks.

The problem of fraternity social host liability in Pennsylvania has been commented upon by Edwin L. Scherlis, Esq., a senior partner at Margolis, Edelstein and Scherlis in Philadelphia. One of his specialties is the defense of liquor liability claims on behalf of social hosts, fraternities and commercial establishments, and the following is published with his permission after personal communication.

"One would be hard pressed in this day and age to overlook the rites of passage at most university fraternities. The consumption of alcoholic beverages has long been associated with fraternity life on the campuses of our universities in this country and only recently has there been an effort made to curtail the overwhelming problem of alcohol abuse among our young citizens. Whether this has been successful or not is not known to this writer and is best left to experts in that area. However, alcohol abuse and the problem it creates has become a predominant social issue in this country. As a result, the judicial decisions involving fraternities and the consumption of alcohol continue to develop.

It was not until 1983 that the Pennsylvania Supreme Court permitted a recovery in a social host liability situation. In the landmark decision of *Congini v. Portersville Valve Com-*

pany [48], the cause of action against a social host who supplied intoxicants to a minor guest was recognized. In that case, Mark Congini was an eighteen-year-old employee of the defendant who attended a party sponsored by his employer. He became intoxicated and then drove off only to become involved in a serious accident which left him permanently disabled. The Supreme Court of Pennsylvania which had earlier refused to extend social host liability for adult intoxicated individuals reasoned that the legislature had made a "legislative judgment that persons under twenty-one years of age are competent to handle alcohol." The legislative judgment was manifested in the section of the Crimes Code which made it a summary criminal offense for an underage person to purchase, consume or possess alcoholic beverages. As will be seen later, another section of the Pennsylvania Crimes Code is important since it penalizes an "accomplice" who participates in the furnishing of alcohol to minors.

The *Congini* court stated that underlying those criminal provisions is the public policy to protect minors and the public at large. Because there is a violation of a statute involved, the Court felt that the host would be "negligent per se," if alcohol was served, to the point of intoxication, to a person less than twenty-one years of age and the social host could be held liable for the injuries proximately resulting from that minor's intoxication. The key to the situation is the furnishing of the intoxicating beverages to a class of persons which the legislature has determined to be incompetent. Interestingly, the Supreme Court held that a minor can be found comparatively negligent, under the Pennsylvania Comparative Negligence Act, for the drinking. The Court felt that an eighteen-year-old person is presumptively capable of negligence and further, by knowingly consuming alcohol, the eighteen year old person is also guilty of committing a summary offense."

It did not take the court long to become involved in the situation where a minor was drinking at a fraternity reception. In *Jefferis v.*

Commonwealth of Pennsylvania and Theta Chi Fraternity (49), Jefferis, a minor, was injured after consuming liquor at the local chapter of the Theta Chi Fraternity. The fraternity claimed that it should not be held liable since there was no evidence available that a fraternity member actually served the minor with the alcohol. The Court noted that if the person who actually served the alcohol was not identified, the theory of liability must then be based on the fact that the defendant may have an "accomplice" of the person who actually served the alcohol. It was found that accomplice liability attaches to those actors who either furnished the alcohol to the minor or promoted that end. The Court found that the following test should be utilized to determine the extent of liability in a social host situation involving an intoxicated minor:

1) The defendant must have intended to act in such a way as to furnish, agree to furnish or promote the furnishing of alcohol to the minor, and

2) The defendant must have acted in a way which did furnish, agree to furnish or promote the furnishing of alcohol to the minor, and

3) The defendant's act must have been a substantial factor in furnishing, agreeing to furnish or the promoting of alcohol to the minor.

The issue thus identified by the *Jefferis* court is whether the facts demonstrated that either the local fraternity or national fraternity provided substantial assistance to the minor in his consumption of alcohol.

Perhaps the most celebrated case involving fraternity activities and responsibilities in this area was decided by the United States Court of Appeals for the Third Circuit in *Fasset v. Villanova Chapter of Delta Kappa Epsilon and its Individual Members, et al.* (50). The fraternity at Villanova University voted to finance a party at the apartment rented by one or more of the fraternity members. An eighteen-year- old guest at the party was served intoxicating liquor, after which he drove his vehicle and was involved in an accident leaving one passenger dead and another severely crippled. The action filed against the driver soon led to the involvement of both the local and national fraternity. Since it was not determined who actually served the drinks to the minor, the Court endeavored to determine whether those who organized and participated in the planning of the party should have legal obligations as "accomplices." The United States Court of Appeals for the Third Circuit was obliged to "anticipate" how the Pennsylvania Supreme Court would decide the same issue and in doing so, summarized the law describing the civil responsibility of those who provided or participated in the provision of alcohol to minors. The Court rejected the concept that only those who "furnished" the liquor could be held responsible and then attempted to define the terms "aiding, agreeing or attempting to aid" in the minor's consumption of alcohol in light of civil liability standards. The Court found that the following factors as suggested by the *Restatement of Torts* will assist the Court in determining whether the assistance rendered by an accomplice should be considered "substantial," since substantiality is essential to a finding of liability:

1) The nature of the act encouraged;

2) The amount of assistance given by the defendant;

3) The defendant's presence or absence at the time of the tort;

4) The defendant's relation to the other tortfeasors;

5) The defendant's state of mind; and

6) The foreseeability of the harm that occurred.

The Court went on to find that those who actually helped organize the party and supplied the alcoholic beverages or the place where the alcoholic beverages were being served actually met the requirements and would be held as accomplices and responsible for the consequences of the intoxication of the minor.

In *Fasset*, all the fraternity members were joined as parties to the litigation. For the most part, each was represented by counsel designated by the homeowner insurance policy maintained by the student or the parents of that student.

Based on these decisions, it became clear that if a local fraternity, through its officers, permitted underage drinking on the premises, the local fraternity and those who were responsible for it certainly face responsibility under the combination of factors suggested by the *Restatement* and cited in *Fasset*.

Neither the *Fasset* nor the *Jefferis* Court really considered the potential liability of the national chapter which, in most cases, maintains a close allegiance with the local chapter and, by contract or other document maintains a significant right of control over the local chapter, its officers and members. This issue was brought before the Pennsylvania Supreme Court in *Alumni Association v. Sullivan* (51). In that case, an eighteen-year-old freshman at Bucknell University attended a party at the Sigma Chi Fraternity where alcohol was served and was openly consumed by him. The minor became intoxicated and negligently caused a fire in the fraternity house resulting in substantial damage. In a suit against the minor, the university, the local fraternity and the national fraternity were joined to the action. The lower court dismissed the claim and the Supreme Court was asked to review the issue of liability. The Court noted that the allegations against the University merely suggested that the school was aware of the activities at the fraternity house and should have prevented them from happening. There was no averment that the school was in any way responsible for supplying, serving or dispensing the alcoholic beverages. Similarly, there were no allegations that the national fraternity had actual knowledge of the activities of the local chapter or the ability of the national fraternity to control such activities.

In dismissing the claim against the university and the national fraternity *Sullivan* Court acknowledged the *Fasset* theory that those who were actively involved in the planning and conduct of the affair in which the intoxicating beverages were served could be held liable along with those who "knowingly furnished" the intoxicants to the minor, However, the Court would not impose a custodial responsibility upon the University and cited from an earlier opinion in *Bradshaw v. Rawlins* (52):

> Our beginning point is the recognition that the modern American college is not an insurer of the safety of its students. Whatever may have been its responsibility in an earlier era, the authoritarian role of today's college administra-

tions has been notably diluted in recent decades. Trustees, administrators, and faculties have been required to yield to the expanding rights and privileges of their students.

The Court held that the college did not stand *in loco parentis* for all its students and thus would jot be held liable for the unfortunate consequences of a minor drinking at a local fraternity house.

It was equally clear to the Court that the national fraternities are also based on a fraternal rather than a paternal relationship. It was noted that the national organizations do not have the ability to monitor the activities of the respective chapters and therefore national fraternities do not assume a duty to closely monitor the social activities of the local fraternities.

The *Sullivan* Court finally stated:

> Fraternal organizations are premised upon a fellowship of equals; it is not a relationship where one group is superior to the other and may be held responsible for the conduct of the other. From this factual matrix, there is no basis in the relationship to expand and the liability of the national body to include responsibility for the conduct of one of its chapters.

Recently, the Pennsylvania Superior Court had an opportunity to render an opinion in a case where an eighteen-year-old was served alcoholic beverages at a Lamda Chi Alpha fraternity house and when driving home was killed in a motor vehicle accident (53). He was legally intoxicated at the time. The suit was brought against the college which was the owner and lessor of the local fraternity house where the drinking took place. The suit was also brought against the national fraternity.

Although it was noted that 70% of the campus was under the legal drinking age and the local fraternity was allowed to build a bar with the service of alcoholic beverages, the Court still did not find a duty owed by either the college or the national fraternity. It was noted that the national fraternity and the college had issued directives to preclude underage drinking. Summary judgment in favor of both the school and the national fraternity was appropriate since it was found that neither entity had the ability to control the behavior of the students as they might have a century before. It was also suggested that no amount of control or supervision by the college could reasonably have been expected to preclude the drinking that took place.

Just when we thought the appropriate formula had been reached to determine whether fraternities, schools, or students would have liability where a minor was injured or injured another after being served intoxicants, the Pennsylvania Superior Court in a majority panel decision decided *Goldberg v. Delta Tau Delta* (54), and a companion case decided the same day *Heller* (55). In *Goldberg*, the minor student attended a fraternity party where she drank, and subsequently spent time over the next twenty-four hours with fellow students where additional drinking and drug abuse took place. They then drove to another fraternity party where she and friends continued to drink and smoke marijuana. The minor, Stella Goldberg, was then escorted from the fraternity house by one of the other students who murdered her. The suit contended that the fraternity was responsible for the minor fraternity members who served the minor decedent. The Court held that the intoxication and drug abuse was limited to the three or four young people who were involved and not the entire fraternity.

The Court then ruled:

> "Therefore, a minor cannot, as a matter of law, be held liable as a social host for furnishing alcoholic beverages to another minor..."

The Court went on to also conclude that various factors which would lead a fraternity to become responsible for such an act were not present in this case. It was also noted that the activity of one fraternity member in providing the decedent with a glass of beer would be considered *de minimus* and certainly would not lead to liability on the part of the local fraternity. The *Goldberg* case has been appealed to the Pennsylvania Supreme Court and it is the opinion of this writer that the Supreme Court will overrule the *Goldberg* opinion and find that a person over eighteen years of age who is responsible for either furnishing or aiding and abetting the furnishing of alcoholic beverages to a person under twenty-one years of age can be held civilly for the damage legally caused by the technical violation of the law.

In summary, local fraternities can certainly be held as accomplices and abettors if they, through their principals, permit minors to be served on the fraternity premises or on another remise with fraternity blessing. However, the national fraternity, which does not exert great control over the local chapter, and which has promulgated and published its statement or policy against underage drinking, will not be held liable in most of these cases."

AVOIDING THIRD PARTY LIABILITY SUITS

Suits against bars, restaurants, clubs and hotels who serve alcohol to intoxicated patrons are extremely common, and the potential losses are incredibly severe. There is a very real risk that unless proprietors of bars, restaurants and hotels respond to this problem they will, at the very least risk loss of their liquor licenses, and, in cases where drunk drivers kill or maim innocent bystanders, the losses could result in possible ruin for those found responsible.

Society has determined that those who hold liquor licenses to serve alcohol for profit have an obligation to the community. The theories of liquor liability involve, in some states, Dram Shop legislation, while in other states, the common-law theory of recovery through negligence applies. It is very easy for juries to understand the establishment's liability in these cases, and they often award huge damages against those found liable. It is therefore absolutely essential that places where alcohol is served develop an atmosphere and control system to minimize any suggestions of negligence. This will not only protect the individual bar owner, but also represents a very important contribution to the public health of the community.

The ultimate test in these cases is always that of reasonableness; that is, how reasonable is the establishment in selling alcohol in a responsible manner. There are several measures in this regard that should be considered.

What advertising, if any, the bar employs to attract customers is of potential importance. For example, a bar that advertises a Happy Hour with cheap drinks, or two drinks for the price of one, should think very seriously of how this might be used by a plaintiff's attorney in influencing the jury that the bar was negligent. If an atmosphere is promoted that encourages drinking to excess, there is no question that this bar will be seen as being irresponsible. However, if the bar, for example, advertises the availability of food to be served along with the alcohol, this can be viewed as a more responsible environment in which alcohol is served. Thus while a Happy Hour consisting of food and alcohol could be viewed as acceptable, serving two drinks for the price of one, especially with no provision of food, could be very difficult to justify.

Another area for bars to consider is the general atmosphere of the establishment. A simple phenomenon, such as the availability of sufficient light has been of importance in cases in which the author has been involved as an expert. When the bar is very dark, especially where there are booths that are usually even darker, it is almost impossible for the bartender to observe patrons for signs of visible intoxication. This proved to be the downfall of one bar in Philadelphia which was successfully sued in a Dram Shop case when the plaintiff's attorney demonstrated to the jury that it was impossible for the bartender to have seen the individuals in a particular booth who he stated were not served while visibly intoxicated. Customers in the next booth testified to the contrary. As well as the availability of sufficient light, a bar would be well advised to provide things for the customers to do other than drink alcohol. The availability of a dart board, video and other games might well persuade the jury that the bar was not only interested in plying the customers with alcohol, but also provided activities that helped to slow down the drinking, and perhaps reduce the amount of alcohol consumed.

The serving of food in any drinking establishment is extremely important from a physiological point of view, as the presence of food in the stomach will significantly slow down the absorption of alcohol. Also, when a patron is eating, it is less likely that he will also be drinking, so that the amount of time spent consuming alcohol will be reduced. It is far better to serve food with a high protein and fat content than simply pretzels and potato chips. The latter do very little other than to increase thirst, but having cheeses, chicken wings, etc. available will have a much more significant impact on reducing alcohol absorption. Whenever possible, the bar should provide and serve such foods in addition to the drinks that they sell. It is far cheaper to provide these free of charge than face the much costlier possibility of a negligence suit. Also, the provision of such food can help persuade a jury that the bar was indeed attempting to be reasonable in the way that it sold alcohol, and trying to prevent intoxication.

The bar should be able to demonstrate its ability and intention to refuse service to underage drinkers, be alert to identifying fake identification cards and confiscating them. Bartenders should be directed to limit the amount of alcohol in each drink and discouraged from serving doubles. It must be remembered that many employees of bars are transient and therefore training must be repeated frequently. Every bartender, waiter and waitress should also receive training in recognizing and responding to signs of visible intoxication. A concise, written statement of policy, including having attended a training program dealing with these issues should be signed by every employee, and a copy inserted in their personnel file.

In order to further promote an atmosphere that encourages responsibility, the establishment should strategically place posters advertising awareness of the dangers of drinking and driving. Messages, such as "Friends Don't Let Friends Drive Drunk" or "Don't Drink and Drive" could be publicized on buttons worn by the employees and on signs on tables and the bar, along with promotions of Mothers and Students Against Drunk Driving. All these suggestions would have a very real impact in reducing drinking and driving, and for an attorney representing the bar, provide a very persuasive argument to a jury that the bar had indeed been reasonable in its attempt to sell alcohol to its patrons responsibly.

The staff of bars and restaurants should be sensitized to think of drinking and driving as an issue that might well involve them personally. For example, the next child killed in a drunk driving accident could be the son or daughter of the proprietor of the bar, the bartender, a waiter or waitress. Similar distress and grief would be experienced if the deceased were a neighbor, relative or friend. Perhaps thinking in this way, a proprietor of a bar or restaurant would be more likely to institute measures discussed, with the almost certain consequence of minimizing cases against the bar.

As mentioned, it is mandatory that all employees involved in the selling of alcohol, in any establishment, should be intensively trained in the recognition of drunkenness. If this training is not given, and documented to have been so, it will demand the critical attention of any plaintiff's attorney. Reasonable efforts must be made to ensure that alcohol is never served to underage drinkers, or to those individuals who are visibly intoxicated. The best attempts by any bar or restaurant will not guarantee success, but it must be remembered that the test is not of guarantee, but of reasonableness.

It is reasonable to suppose that customers drinking alcohol in a bar or restaurant do so to relax, to interact pleasurably with others, and to feel a sense of happiness. These are perfectly acceptable reactions that one would expect to observe in people drinking alcohol in any establishment, and there is no expectation that this behavior should not be condoned and encouraged. It can indeed be promoted by providing free snacks and having various activities available in the bar to slow down the drinking process. This behavior is "normal" in these settings, and not thought of as being visibly intoxicated.

Unfortunately, in too many individuals, this type of drinking behavior is not maintained, and symptoms begin to appear that should warn a vigilant bartender, waiter or waitress, that problems might be developing. Commonly, the drinker becomes overly friendly, acts overconfidently, becomes rather careless or gets involved in unusual behavior, such as arm wrestling. Sometimes, a degree of loudness or bragging might be observed, and a well-trained, observant bartender will begin to pay more attention to individuals with any of these behavior patterns. Intervention at this stage might be to offer snacks, water or other non-alcoholic drinks to these individuals. These behaviors certainly demand a higher degree of vigilance, and a close eye should be kept on these persons for the development of more obvious signs of intoxication. It is often possible at this stage to encourage them to slow down or stop their drinking, and staff should be encouraged to intervene to the best of their ability at this time.

The next stage of alcohol intoxication is characterized by signs and symptoms that place the individual in an unqualified danger zone. These symptoms include extreme boisterousness, belligerence and argumentativeness. Loss of inhibitory control frequently results in sexual lewdness and frequent loud obscenities. Speech becomes obviously slurred and there is loud, inappropriate laughter. There is often extreme emotional lability with crying jags interspersed with jocularity. Muscular coordination becomes impaired, with typical signs being the spilling of drinks, or clumsiness and inability to light a cigarette. Patrons often throw money around, insist on buying rounds for the whole bar, or ordering doubles or triples. Judgment is seriously impaired, the eyes might appear extremely reddened, there is unsteadiness, and tripping or falling might occur. The individual has difficulty picking up change, is obviously forgetful, and might even fall asleep at the bar or at the table.

When any of these danger symptoms are observed, the bartender or other employees should immediately bring this individual to the attention of the manager. At this point, alcohol should no longer be served, and there should be an absolutely clear understanding that the manager will support this decision when it is made by an employee. This process should be carried out diplomatically so that customers are not insulted, as this might make them even more belligerent. The intent is not to embarrass the patron, but under no circumstances should any further alcohol be served. Many individuals will respond positively to firm, soft speech, and the offer of food and non-alcoholic beverages. Arrangements should be in place to offer free parking, a ride home if necessary, or to pay for a cab. Any cost involved is trivial compared with the very real risk of such an individual leaving the bar in an obvious state of intoxication and operating a motor vehicle.

Every bar, restaurant, hotel or any establishment selling alcoholic beverages is risking financial disaster if it does not have a comprehensive plan and policy based on these principles. As stated, it must be in writing, and employees should sign a statement spelling out their understanding of the plan, their involvement in a training program to identify intoxicated patrons and their responsibilities and duties in such cases. The personnel file of every employee should contain this signed and dated statement. Having these measures in place will make the task of an attorney defending the establishment in a third party liability suit much easier.

In addition to the *Boudwin* case (47) which has been described in detail, several other cases have been litigated and help to demonstrate their complexity and diversity.

While bars and restaurants are the usual establishments charged with serving patrons while visibly intoxicated, one very interesting case involved a baseball fan who was consuming beer during a Philadelphia Phillies game at Veterans Stadium in Philadelphia. This man consumed a quantity of beer during the course of the game and, after leaving the stadium, was involved in a motor vehicle accident that resulted in the death of two of his companions. A suit was brought against the owners of the franchise that was responsible for selling alcohol to the fan while he was visibly intoxicated. This individual had a blood alcohol level of .15% at the time of the accident, and had been observed to be rather boisterous during the course of the game. However, the jury was persuaded that his behavior at the ballpark did not differ significantly from the majority of other Philadelphia baseball fans who are, more often than not, in a state of boisterousness and obvious excitement. It could not be shown that this particular fan demonstrated any behavior that made him stand out from the kind of behavior that would be regarded as normal in this setting, and he was therefore not considered to be in a state of visible intoxication. The case does, however, demonstrate that sports stadiums also have a responsibility in not selling alcohol to visibly intoxicated individuals.

The importance of considering the medical examination of the plaintiff in these cases is illustrated by the following. Mr. V was involved in a motor vehicle accident when the car which he was driving overturned. He was taken from the scene of the accident to a local hospital, and examined in the emergency room at that hospital about forty minutes after the accident. The medical record noted that he was not wearing a seatbelt at the time of the accident, and admitted to drinking four mixed drinks containing gin and tonic. He had been transported to the hospital on a backboard wearing a cervical collar, and was conscious when the rescue personnel arrived at the accident scene. The patient was uncertain whether he had lost consciousness.

He was noted to be mildly confused, uncertain of his age, and had sustained a laceration of his left forehead. There were also abrasions of his right head and face, as well as his right thigh. He was obviously able to answer questions, was oriented to time and place, and there was no mention in the medical record that he was slurring his speech. There was however, mention that his conjunctivae were injected, but no observation was made that they were markedly reddened. There was also no comment made in the record that he was in any way overtly intoxicated. His serum alcohol level, however, was .27%.

Because of the lack of a CT Scanner at this hospital, he was transferred to one of the university hospitals, and arrived there at 2:30 A.M., four and a half hours after the accident. He was still alert and oriented in all spheres when he arrived at this hospital, and examination by a neurologist noted that he was able to follow all commands, was wide awake and his speech was normal. No observation was made of any undue redness of his conjunctivae, and there was nothing in the examination to suggest that he appeared to be intoxicated. The neurologic examination had specifically ruled out any sensory or motor deficits. The CT Scan was negative, and the plaintiff apparently left the hospital sometime after 2:30 P.M. the same day without waiting to be formally discharged.

Mr. V was known to have been a patron at a very popular drinking establishment in Philadelphia prior to his accident, but the time of his arrival and departure from that establishment were unclear. He testified that he worked that day from 8:00 AM. until 4:00 P.M., and arrived at the bar at about 5:00 P.M. He stated that he and a friend together spent one hundred and twenty dollars while at this bar for drinks, but he is unsure what time he left the bar. One of the waitresses testified that he was only at the bar for about forty minutes, during which time he and his companion had just one round of drinks before leaving. The bartender also remembered that he and his friend had just one drink each, and he recalled them being present at the bar for no longer than twenty minutes. He also testified that had Mr. V and his companion remained in the bar for over four hours, and had Mr. V himself spent sixty dollars on drinks, he would have obviously remembered them. Both the bartender and the cocktail waitress recalled seeing no signs that Mr. V was intoxicated with alcohol while he was present at the bar.

There was testimony from another individual who was present at the bar that evening that he did speak with Mr. V and considered him to be intoxicated. Specifically, he mentioned that Mr. V was slurring his speech and that "his eyes were red as a beet." His comments were obviously in direct conflict with those of the bartender and the cocktail waitress who also observed him that evening and served him the drinks.

It was known that Mr. V's serum alcohol concentration at 11:29 P.M. was measured at the hospital at .27%. His whole blood alcohol concentration was therefore approximately .23%. At the time of this incident, Mr. V weighed 175 lbs and would have needed to consume approximately 12 drinks in the course of one hour or between 14 and 15 drinks over the course of four hours to arrive at this blood alcohol concentration. These drinks would represent one oz of 86-proof alcohol or 12 oz of beer each. If he had consumed this quantity of alcohol while a patron at the bar, it was highly likely that the bartender or the waitress, or both, would have clearly remembered him as a customer that evening. If, as they had both testified, he was only present at the bar for between twenty to forty minutes, it would have been virtually impossible for him to consume this amount of alcohol in that time. With the exception of the one witness, nobody appeared to have noticed any obvious signs of intoxication demonstrated by Mr. V while he was at the bar. If he had consumed only one drink while at this bar, he would have needed to consume a further very large quantity of alcohol to arrive at a blood alcohol concentration of .23% after his admission to the hospital. The fact that he showed no overt or obvious signs of alcohol intoxication when he was examined at this hospital, as well as at the second hospital, would suggest that Mr. V had a very high tolerance for alcohol. The majority of individuals with a blood alcohol concentration of .23% would have been noted to have some signs suggestive of alcohol intoxication.

An opinion was given to the jury that Mr. V did not show any signs of visible intoxication with alcohol while he was being served at the bar. The observation by one witness that he was intoxicated, and had slurred speech and "beet red eyes," was pointed out as not being supported by the observations and examinations by two physicians at different hospitals. The point was made that had these symptoms been present, they would have undoubtedly been noted in the medical examinations, and it could therefore be concluded that, with a blood alcohol level of .23%, Mr. V did not manifest slurring of speech, obvious reddening of his conjunctivae, disturbance of gait, boisterousness or drowsiness. The absence of these phenomena in a medical examination carries great weight with juries, while their presence would be equally significant. Careful examination of the medical records in these cases is therefore of critical importance.

An unusual and intriguing case involving alcohol intoxication, which was widely publicized nationally, was that involving Mr. Leonard Tose, a previous owner of the Philadelphia Eagles Football Team. He had lost an enormous sum of money gambling in a casino in Atlantic City, New Jersey, and he was sued by the casino when he defaulted on part of his gambling debt. Mr. Tose in turn sued the casino for allowing him to gamble in an advanced state of alcohol intoxication. He claims that the casino had encouraged him to come and gamble by sending limousines and helicopters to transport him from Philadelphia to Atlantic City. They provided him with his own table to play blackjack, and while there made certain that his favorite whiskey was always available in unlimited quantities and, he claims, had encouraged him to continue gambling for extremely large sums while he was in a state of obvious intoxication. Mr. Tose appears to have been addicted to alcohol and witnesses stated that he was frequently in an obvious state of intoxication while gambling at the casino.

The jury in this case found in favor of the casino, and did not consider the losses incurred by Mr. Tose while intoxicated as being the responsibility of the establishment providing the alcohol. Casinos, however, like other establishments providing alcohol, are liable under the Dram Shop Act, and would be well advised to take extraordinary measures to assure that no patron is served alcohol while in a state of visible intoxication.

8

EXPERT PSYCHIATRIC TESTIMONY
IN DRUNK DRIVING CASES

There are several issues involved in the litigation of these cases that should be considered by both prosecuting and defense attorneys. Objective, comprehensive, and accurate assessment of the drunk driving suspect is of paramount importance.

Because these subjects, by definition, are thought to be intoxicated with alcohol, and possibly other drugs, a medical examination of these individuals prior to their being incarcerated is often, but not always, carried out. This medical examination by a physician is often important in determining the presence or absence of objective signs of intoxication. Physicians carrying out these examinations should be knowledgeable and experienced in the assessment of intoxicated behavior and the examination should not be cursory, but comprehensive and detailed. Particular attention must be given to the exclusion of other conditions that might mimic alcohol intoxication, particularly injuries to the head or metabolic disorders, such as diabetes mellitus. Doctors are often questioned by defense attorneys as to whether the suspect would have been unable to perform the various sobriety tests, even if he had consumed no alcohol, and any other conditions that can cause intoxication symptoms should be looked for in the history and examination.

Most police departments have standardized forms for the sobriety examinations completed by physicians. On these forms, the pulse, blood pressure and temperature of the suspects should always be noted. Unless the degree of intoxication is extremely severe, these three vital signs are usually not adversely affected by alcohol. If any of them are abnormal, other possible medical reasons for the apparent intoxication should be suspected. Further, it needs to be emphasized that normal blood pressure, pulse and temperature in no way contradict the presence of intoxication.

There are a great number of conditions that might cause similar or identical symptoms to those found in persons who are diagnosed as being intoxicated with alcohol or other drugs. For example, facial flushing can be due to a pre-existing ruddy complexion, extreme shyness or embarrassment, some cases of gastric hyperacidity, and occasionally hypertension. Slurring of speech can be the result of various neurologic diseases including cerebrovascular accidents, multiple sclerosis, brain tumors or abscesses. Also, extreme anxiety and local pathology of the mouth or tongue can result in speech impediments that are similar to those found in intoxicated persons.

The impairment of muscular coordination seen in intoxication which results in clumsiness, stumbling and falling, can also be found in association with a large number of medical diseases. Disorders of equilibrium and gait are seen in patient's with hemiparesis, Parkinson's disease and particularly in diseases of the cerebellum. A characteristic gait disorder, known as sensory ataxia, results from a loss of sensation in the lower extremities due to disease processes on the peripheral nerves, dorsal roots, dorsal columns of the spinal cord or the medial lemnisci. Cerebral palsy, most of the cases resulting from hypoxic injury to the nervous system in the perinatal period, invariably produces gait disturbances, and patients with choreic movements often develop a characteristic disorder of gait. Various forms of muscular dystrophy, frontal lobe disease, normal pressure hydrocephalus and multiple sclerosis are also often associated with ataxia and incoordination. Other central nervous system depressant drugs can also result in slurring of speech and muscular incoordination; these include hypnotics, benzodiazepines, barbiturates, opiates and sometimes psychotropics and antidepressants.

It should not be forgotten that aging often results in changes in gait and difficulties with balance. Thus, the elderly drunk driver deserves particular attention when making an assessment of intoxication. Lower motor neurone disease and hysterical gait disorders must also be included in the differential diagnosis of intoxication.

Sophisticated litigation of the drunk driver must take into consideration this large group of medical and neurologic diseases that can result in symptoms identical with those found in alcohol and drug intoxication. The presence or exclusion of these disorders can be of assistance to prosecuting and defense attorneys and the forensic psychiatrist must be familiar with the complexities in assessing these cases.

Surprisingly, there have been cases of drunk driving defended on the basis of pleading not guilty by reason of insanity. These have usually been alcoholics who were successful in their professions and retained considerable finances. They were repeat drunk driving offenders who were subject to incarceration for long periods of time if they were again convicted for driving under the influence of alcohol. Rather than plead guilty or not guilty to the drunk driving charge, their attorneys had chosen to try an insanity plea. In order to make this kind of defense work, it is essential to obtain the opinion from a physician that the first consumption of alcohol by the defendant was an involuntary act. Having elicited this opinion, the rule that intoxication is no defense to a criminal act, may be neutralized. The diagnosis of alcoholism must be established and in some of these cases there have also been other psychiatric diagnoses and physical complaints, such as hypoglycemia. Under these circumstances, juries have found these defendants not guilty of drunk driving by reason of insanity.

It should be noted that many medicines contain a significant quantity of ethyl alcohol with some concentrations in these preparations being as high as 68%. Over-the-counter cough medicines can contain as much as 20% alcohol, and therefore the blood alcohol concentration in a particular defendant might be explained on the basis of his having taken, or been prescribed, medications that are high in alcohol content. Special inquiry as to what medications the defendant took prior to the arrest can be extremely important in litigating these cases.

The author has been involved in several cases where defendants have been arrested for driving while intoxicated, who were found to have psychiatric symptoms that were being treated with antidepressant medications and anxiolytic drugs. In conjunction with alcohol, these drugs often exaggerate the degree of intoxication, and judges have been generally sympathetic to individuals who have an established psychiatric diagnosis and whose drinking might be seen as part of this process. When the presence of alcohol dependence can also be established, there is an increased likelihood that the courts will accept alternative dispositions to incarceration or license revocation. Where illicit drugs have been used, however, the courts have shown much less tolerance, and have often been more severe in applying sanctions

CASE VIGNETTES

Case 1

Cases in which driving while intoxicated has led to significant property damage, physical injuries or death are common examples of the cases that the author has been asked to act in as an expert. A fairly typical case was one in which a car was involved in an accident with a Yellow Cab. This accident occurred at an intersection in Philadelphia when the driver of the car was returning from the Jersey shore. While there, the driver had purchased a quantity of beer, and testified that he consumed two, 12-oz. bottles of beer with his lunch between 12:00 and 12:30 P.M. He further testified that he had consumed no more beer after leaving Ocean City for Philadelphia between 12:30 and 1:00 P.M. Following the accident, the driver and his companion were taken to the Hospital of the University of Pennsylvania for treatment. The emergency room nurse's record stated that the driver admitted to consuming alcohol, had an odor of alcohol on his breath, and "was drunk." A sample of his blood drawn at 5:10 P.M. had an alcohol concentration of .159% in the serum.

The author, testifying on behalf of the Yellow Cab Company, testified that this serum alcohol level was equivalent to a whole blood alcohol concentration of .13%. He also indicated that the accident had occurred at 3:15 P.M., which was two hours before his blood alcohol concentration was found to be .13%. Since it is known that alcohol is metabolized in the body at an average rate of about .018% per hour, the driver's blood alcohol concentration at the time of the accident was calculated to have been about .17%.

The expert's report and testimony demonstrated that it would require the amount of alcohol contained in about eight or nine, 12-oz. bottles of beer to produce a blood alcohol concentration of .17%.

The author testified that in his opinion, at the time of the accident, the driver of the automobile had a blood alcohol concentration of .17%, and was intoxicated with alcohol to an extent that he was incapable of safely operating an automobile. It was also pointed out that the observation by the nurse, in the emergency room at the Hospital of the University of Pennsylvania, that the individual was drunk was absolutely consistent with his blood alcohol level. Testimony emphasized that this blood alcohol level of .17% would have produced marked impairment of judgment, and the driver's inhibitory control and restraint would have been markedly relaxed. It was also stated that his muscular coordination and control would have been severely impaired, and his reaction time slowed down. It was explained to the judge and jury that reaction time is that time elapsing between receipt of a visual or auditory stimulus and the reaction to it, which, in a sober person is no more than one-tenth of a second. while intoxicated with alcohol at .17%, it would take about a quarter to a half a second to respond.

The jury was also informed that, at this blood alcohol level, the driver would have had marked distortion of time and space, so that distances traveled would be perceived by him as being much shorter than they really were, and events would appear to be happening much more slowly than they were. Further, it was pointed out that alcohol at this level would have also have affected his ability to differentiate between colors.

The jury was educated to the fact that at a blood alcohol level of .17% there is considerable depression of the central nervous system with a very strong likelihood of drowsiness, lethargy and lack of alertness. It was therefore asserted that the driver of the automobile, with a blood alcohol level of .17%, was in no condition to safely drive his car when he was involved in the accident with the yellow cab. It was expressed, within a reasonable degree of medical certainty, that this blood alcohol concentration, .17%, was a highly significant factor in the causation of this accident.

The author's testimony was accepted by the jury, and the driver of the Yellow Cab exonerated from all responsibility. Since there were very serious medical injuries and property damage in this accident, potential loss to the Yellow Cab Company was appreciable, and the presentation of the facts in the way described convinced the jury to find in favor of the defendant. The blood alcohol level was the major factor in determining that the driver of the automobile had clearly lied about the amount of alcohol consumed and when he had consumed it.

Case 2

Another case involved an accident that occurred about 2:30 A.M. in November, 1987 when Mr. TF was seriously injured when he was struck by a car driven by Mr. TSB. TF was operating a tractor trailer that he had parked, and he was apparently in the process of climbing from the cab when he was struck while on the running board of the tractor. He was taken to Albert Einstein Medical Center, where it was noted that he had been caught between the car and the tractor trailer, and his left lower extremity had been severed. While in the emergency room at the hospital, a sample of his blood was found to have a serum alcohol content of .142% and his urine contained opiates and cocaine. The blood alcohol concentration is approximately 15% less than the alcohol concentration in the serum, so that TF's blood alcohol concentration while in the emergency room was .12%.

It was noted that this was above the level designated as being legally intoxicated to operate an automobile in the Commonwealth of Pennsylvania. In a statement given on May 27, 1988, TF denied drinking any alcohol or taking any other drugs at the time of the accident, but the results of his blood and urine studies in the emergency room clearly indicated that this was not the case. His blood alcohol level of .12% showed that there was the equivalent of at least 6 oz of alcohol circulating in his blood at the time of the accident, and the presence of opiates and cocaine in his urine was conclusive proof that both these drugs were present in his system at the time of the accident. There was no question that the alcohol content of .12%, in and of itself, would have produced significant impairment. It was pointed out that judgment becomes impaired with a blood alcohol level of about .04% and, as the blood alcohol level rises, further symptoms and signs of impairment of the central nervous system become increasingly apparent.

The report in this case stated that at .08% there are beginning signs of unsteadiness, and muscular control and coordination become impaired at a blood alcohol level between .10% and .12%. Quite commonly at this stage, thoughts can become confused, and tripping and stumbling can occur. In addition to the alcohol present in his body, there was also a quantity of cocaine, as well as an opiate. It was pointed out that both these drugs have direct effects on the brain which can produce further impairment in judgment and, depending on the quantity, neuromuscular coordination problems and general brain dysfunction. The author concluded that this combination of alcohol, opiates and cocaine, would have certainly impacted on TF's ability to operate the tractor trailer safely.

It was stated that he would have been far less likely to be able to exercise good judgment in so far as where he would park his vehicle, ensure that his lights were turned on, and be aware of potential hazards. With a blood alcohol concentration of .12%, his reaction time would have been appreciably slower, and he would therefore have been less likely to have been able to avoid potentially dangerous situations. The author's opinion was, within a reasonable degree of medical certainty, that in the early morning hours of November 11, 1987, TF was significantly impaired as a result of the presence of alcohol, opiates and cocaine in his blood, and the impairment was a substantial contributory factor to the accident that occurred.

Case 3

An interesting case of drunk driving that was successfully litigated involved the issue of intent. An automobile driven by Mr. TB struck Ms. RH and possibly her companion, Mr. OH, and Ms. RH later died from the injuries sustained. Ms. RH and Mr. OH were walking on the sidewalk, when a car operated by TB mounted the sidewalk and struck at least Ms. RH. TB and Ms. RH were both taken to a local hospital where TB's blood alcohol level was found to be .30%.

TB was eventually prosecuted and convicted of first-degree murder. The author testified that while TB was obviously intoxicated with alcohol, his actions on the night of the accident were such that he was able to form the intent to strike the pedestrian. It was stated that there was no reason to suppose that a blood alcohol level of .30% prevented TB from knowing what he was doing, and he was capable of driving his car, exiting and re-entering the vehicle, and then driving it onto the sidewalk and striking the pedestrian. This suggested that TB had considerable tolerance to alcohol and it was the expert's opinion, within a reasonable degree of medical certainty, that he was fully capable of forming the intent to strike and kill Ms. RH in spite of a blood alcohol level of .30%.

Case 4

Another interesting case was one in which the author reviewed the police accident report and the toxicology report from the Philadelphia Police Department Criminalistics Laboratory regarding a case in which the Commonwealth of Pennsylvania was being sued. On December 19, 1985, at 2:02 A.M., a car driven by Mr. GH entered an exit ramp from the Roosevelt Expressway and collided with another car driven by Mr. VS that was proceeding legally in a southbound direction on the extension. VS stated that while driving in the center lane at between forty and forty-five miles per hour, he was suddenly confronted by the headlights of the car driven by GH coming up the exit ramp in the wrong direction and then had no further memory of the accident.

When GH was interviewed in the emergency room of the Medical College of Pennsylvania Hospital, he appeared to have had no recollection of the accident. When asked to explain the accident that he had been involved in, his answer was "What accident?" When specifics of the accident were explained his response was "I don't know what you are talking about." During this interview, it was noted that a strong odor of alcohol was emanating from GH and a sample of his blood drawn at 2:52 A.M. was found to contain alcohol in a concentration of .28%.

In order to calculate what GH's blood alcohol level would have been at 2:02 A.M., which was the time of the accident, it was necessary to know the time that he consumed his last drink. Since that was known, it was uncertain whether his blood alcohol concentration was rising or falling at the time of the accident. Had he consumed most of his alcohol in taking his last drink shortly before the accident, his blood alcohol level at 2:02 A.M. would have been about .29%. At either of these levels, and within the range of approximately .26 to .29%., GH was grossly intoxicated with alcohol at the time of the accident.

It was the author's opinion that when this accident occurred, GH, with a blood alcohol level of between .26 and .29%, would have been markedly confused, would have lost all sense of judgment, and was in such a condition of central nervous system depression that he would have been totally incapable of safely walking, let alone operating an automobile. At this blood alcohol level, his coordination and balance were severely impaired, his reflex responses were extremely slow, and his judgment of speed and distance was profoundly compromised. Awareness of what he was seeing, hearing or doing was significantly impaired, and he would have been totally incapable of responding correctly to warning or directional signs of even a simple nature.

The expert's report also made reference to GH's response to questions following the accident, and his apparent inability to recall that there had been an accident. The opinion was given that this inability to recall the accident was perfectly consistent with the fact that he was profoundly intoxicated with a blood alcohol level between .26 and .29%. The conclusion was that GH's intoxication with alcohol was the sole cause of his driving in the wrong direction up an exit ramp and colliding with a car driven by VS on the Roosevelt Expressway. The jury accepted the expert testimony as described above and the Commonwealth of Pennsylvania was freed from all liability in this case.

Case 5

Establishing exactly where, and at what time, alcohol was consumed can be of great significance in drunk driving cases. A case demonstrating this was that in which the author provided an expert opinion to the attorney representing a Chinese restaurant. Mrs. LD, her two children and her younger brother, MM were customers at the Chinese restaurant for between three to four hours, although it was uncertain specifically when they arrived and departed. While at this restaurant, the two adults consumed a quantity of beer and two mixed drinks each, as well as eating a meal. None of them appeared to show any signs of alcohol intoxication while at the restaurant, and there was no evidence that MM was in any way loud or boisterous, unsteady on his feet or showing any signs of lack of coordination. At the time of their departure from the Chinese restaurant, MM was able to walk unassisted to the car and LD seems to have been perfectly comfortable in allowing him to drive away from the restaurant with her and her two children as passengers.

MM was then able to drive the car, accompanied by his sister and her two children, to a local shopping center, and then to a mall where they dropped off the two children at a movie theater. He was able to operate the automobile in a normal and responsible manner for at least an hour after leaving the Chinese restaurant, driving to the two malls and eventually arriving at a tavern at approximately 10:00 P.M.

It was emphasized in the report that whatever alcohol was consumed at the Chinese restaurant did not appear to have in any way affected MM's driving performance during this time.

Following their arrival at the tavern, MM consumed a quantity of beer as well as shots of liquor, and continued to drink alcohol in spite of his sister asking him to leave. He became loud and hostile, and apparently spilled someone's drink. They eventually left this tavern together, following which his driving became so uncontrolled that his sister insisted on getting out of the car. Sometime later, it was reported that she was struck by another vehicle and seriously injured.

The report went on to state that at the time of the incident, MM was nineteen years old and had he consumed an appreciable quantity of alcohol at the Chinese restaurant, the expert would have expected him to show some early signs of intoxication. This does not appear to have been the case, and he and LD recall that he showed no signs whatsoever of visible intoxication at that restaurant. The fact that he was able to safely operate an automobile for a considerable period of time between leaving the Chinese restaurant and arriving at the other tavern is proof that whatever alcohol he did consume at the Chinese restaurant was not sufficient to produce any significant impairment. His behavior prior to arrival at the tavern was in no way unusual and he appeared to have been in full control of his faculties. This was in marked contradistinction to the behavior that he manifested while at the tavern, and particularly when operating the automobile after leaving this tavern.

It was the opinion of the author, testifying as an expert, that taking all these facts into consideration, within a reasonable degree of medical certainty, any alcohol consumed by MM at the Chinese restaurant was not a substantial factor in influencing his ability after leaving the tavern, and did not contribute appreciably to the way in which he was reported to be driving at the time LD decided that she should leave the vehicle.

Case 6

The issue of being able to safely operate a motor vehicle is frequently the issue in driving-while-intoxicated cases. On October 28, 1984, Mr. D was driving his motorcycle in a southerly direction on State Road in Philadelphia when he lost control of the vehicle and was thrown from the motorcycle striking the left rear tire of a parked van and sustaining severe injuries. He was taken from the scene of the accident to a local hospital, where he was found to be dead on arrival. The toxicology report showed that at the time of the accident he had a blood alcohol level of .29%.

The expert opinion offered by the author was that at this level of alcohol in his blood, Mr. D was in a severe state of intoxication and would have had markedly impaired coordination, serious lack of judgment and extreme impairment of reflex responses. The legal limit of alcohol in the blood for driving while intoxicated with alcohol is 0.10%, and Mr. D had an alcohol content almost three times the legal limit. It is well accepted clinically that at a blood alcohol level of .10%, and probably even less, the capacity to safely operate a motor vehicle is markedly impaired. There is no doubt whatsoever, therefore, that the blood alcohol concentration of .29% that was present in Mr. D was a major contributory factor to the accident that resulted in his demise.

It was emphasized that safely operating a motorcycle is a very complex task that requires excellent judgment, awareness of road conditions, a high degree of neuromuscular coordination and the ability to see and hear clearly. All these functions were grossly impaired in Mr. D when his blood alcohol level was .29%. It was therefore the opinion of the expert that, within a reasonable degree of medical certainty, the blood alcohol level of .29% found in Mr. D at the time of his death affected his judgment and behavior to such an extent that it caused him to lose control of his motorcycle.

Case 7

Another report regarding an individual who was driving while intoxicated also refers to the importance of alcohol as a contributory factor to an accident. Mr. MC was admitted to a local medical center in May, 1993 suffering from multiple trauma sustained in an accident, when he drove his work truck off the road into a ditch. As a result of his injuries he was rendered paraplegic. He also sustained a head injury with an open, depressed skull fracture, right rib fracture with hemothorax, and fractures of his right second metacarpal bone, the head of his left humerus, a right temporal bone fracture and a frontal sinus fracture. The diagnostic profile at the medical center also included intoxication with alcohol.

In his deposition, MC reported drinking a 12 oz. can of beer at one location between 2:00 and 2:30 P.M., three, 12-oz. cans of beer at a second location approximately twenty minutes later, and just before leaving this bar, one shot of whiskey. This was at approximately 3:45 P.M. and the police accident report notes that the accident occurred at 4:58 P.M. A sample of his blood taken after his arrival at the medical center had a blood alcohol concentration of .137%. This sample of blood is noted in the medical record as having been taken at 6:51 P.M., that is, approximately two hours after the motor vehicle accident.

Assuming that no further alcohol was consumed after he left the second bar, MC's blood alcohol concentration at the time of the accident would have been somewhat higher than the .137% measured at the hospital. The average rate at which alcohol is metabolized per hour is .018% per hour, and at the time of the accident, MC's blood alcohol concentration would have approximated .137% plus 2x 0.18% (0.36%) which is a level of approximately .17%. The percentage of alcohol in his blood was entirely consistent with the hospital diagnosis of alcohol intoxication, and it should be noted that, in the Commonwealth of Pennsylvania, a blood alcohol level of .10% or higher is regarded as legal intoxication.

The opinion was offered that MC's judgment would have become quite obviously impaired at a blood alcohol level much lower than .17%, and at even a level of .04%, judgment already begins to be affected. At the time of this accident, with a blood alcohol level of .17%, his judgment would have been impaired to an extent that he would be reckless, probably drive at excessive speed, and be unable to respond promptly to normal driving hazards. This is because his reaction time would be appreciably slowed, and even if he were aware of an emergency situation, his response time would have been markedly delayed. Also, at this blood alcohol level, his judgment of distance and speed would have been distorted, and the situation would have appeared to have been occurring at a much slower rate than in fact it was. At .17%, he would have had significant impairment of coordination, his reflex responses would have been slowed, and hand-eye coordination particularly impaired. At this blood alcohol concentration, he would have had difficulty walking and balancing, let alone be able to exercise judgment and coordination necessary to operate a complex piece of machinery, such as the truck he was operating. In addition to the symptoms noted, a blood alcohol concentration of .17% would have also resulted in visual impairment with difficulty in differentiating between colors.

Case 8

Alcohol is frequently involved in cases of slips and falls. The estate of RD sued the Philadelphia Housing Authority after he fell down a flight of stairs and was killed. The blood alcohol level at the time of his death was .408%. This man, weighing 190 lbs. would have had to consume approximately twenty-four drinks containing 1 oz. of 86-proof alcohol or 12 oz. of beer to arrive at this blood alcohol level. He would have had severely impaired coordination, balance and judgment. His appreciation of heights or danger would be nonexistent. Such individuals are unable to anticipate dangerous situations, and their reflex responses are so diminished that they cannot take appropriate avoidance reactions, such as stepping away from an object that might be in their way, or avoiding a clearly perilous situation. It would be impossible to safely negotiate a flight of stairs, and it was concluded that his blood alcohol level played a primary role in his falling and dying of his injuries.

Case 9

A case with rather a different twist was that of a thirty-five-year-old white female referred by her attorney for evaluation. She had begun drinking alcohol at the age of fourteen, and by the age of fifteen had experienced her first blackout or alcoholic amnesic episode. She continued to drink regularly and heavily during her teenage years and, by the time she was eighteen years old, was totally dependent on alcohol. From the age of eighteen to twenty-three, she drank virtually on a daily basis, consuming large quantities of alcohol and usually taking her first drink in the early part of the day. She was consuming "anything and everything," and described frequent amnesic episodes after drinking when she would entirely forget what she had done, or where she had been. At the age of seventeen, she briefly used cocaine and methamphetamine, but alcohol remained her primary drug of abuse, and she had not used or abused any drug other than alcohol since the age of nineteen.

She was first admitted to a hospital for the treatment of alcoholism at the age of nineteen when she was a patient for fourteen days. She was discharged and relapsed into drinking almost immediately, and her next hospitalization was for detoxification from alcohol at the age of twenty-two. She was virtually unemployable during these years, was forced to drop out of college, and for some time lived essentially "on the streets." She was obviously extremely dysfunctional during these years and lived with a variety of people who also were alcohol or drug abusers. Her behavior deteriorated to such an extent that when she was twenty-three years old, she entered a long-term rehabilitation program and remained there for five months.

This treatment exposure was successful and after discharge from that program, she remained alcohol-free for eight years, attending meetings of Alcoholics Anonymous frequently and regularly. Four years ago, while on a visit to Malaysia, she relapsed and began drinking again for five days, but was fortunate enough to become associated with Alcoholics Anonymous in Malaysia and again found sobriety and remained in this condition until December, 1993. She had started an extremely successful business and was doing exceptionally well.

She described being in a very close relationship with a man, and when this relationship was threatened, she again relapsed and commenced drinking alcohol. For two days she drank extremely heavily, consuming a combination of wine and beer, and again began to drink in the mornings. On the second day of drinking, she vaguely recalls consuming at least three beers, several shots and part of a bottle of champagne. Her memories of this episode were very vague, but she does recall driving her car and hitting something. Her next clear memory was of waking up in a jail cell four or five hours later.

She had no understanding of why she was in jail, and had no recollection of being arrested or being involved in an accident. She was informed a week later that she had refused to take a Breathalyzer examination. She had no prior arrests, and when she was seen in traffic court she accepted an ARD program and was told that her license had been suspended for a year. She relapsed into drinking for one day a short time later, and became so concerned that she signed herself into a relapse program where she remained for three weeks. Since then, she had been entirely sober, and had again been involved frequently and regularly with Alcoholics Anonymous.

On the basis of the history and examination, there was no question that the diagnosis was chronic alcoholism, and it was evident that this disease began when she was fourteen years old, and continued unabated through her teenage years until she was fortunate enough to find a successful treatment program at the age of twenty-three. Her illness was characterized by the consumption of large quantities of alcohol on a daily basis, drinking in the first part of the day to control anxiety and tremulousness, and the presence of alcoholic "blackouts" or amnesic episodes.

Her disease had progressed, as alcoholism tends to do, although she had many years of sobriety and alcohol-free living. On the occasions when she had relapsed, it was obvious that progression was present, and she developed amnesic episodes after relevantly small quantities of alcohol. This is a characteristic finding in chronic alcoholic patients, and the author expressed his opinion that he had no doubt that her history of the alcoholic "blackout" having occurred when she was arrested was valid. She literally had no memory of having been arrested, or why, and the last event that she recalled was of driving her car and "hitting something." When she was confronted by the police, she was in a state of total amnesia. She was therefore unable to recall being asked to take a Breathalyzer examination, and she had no understanding or comprehension of what this entailed. She would have also been quite incapable of understanding the consequences of not taking such an examination under these circumstances.

It was emphasized to her attorney that one of the characteristics of alcoholism or alcohol dependence is that once a first drink has been taken, most patients find it impossible to control their intake of alcohol and compulsively continue to drink until they are intoxicated or lose consciousness. This patient's history confirmed that this indeed was a symptom that she had, and she was very aware that if any alcohol was consumed, it would invariably lead to a continuing relapse. The disease, in her case, was almost certainly genetically determined, and details of this were provided to the attorney.

The argument in this case was that the patient was in a state of total amnesia and therefore completely incapable of understanding what she was being asked to do by the arresting police officers. As well as having no recall of these events, she was specifically unable to understand the consequences of refusing to take a Breathalyzer examination. It was hoped that this argument would allow her to maintain her driving license which was essential for her work, but as it turned out, the arresting officer failed to attend the hearing and the case was dismissed. If an argument of this kind was to work, the judge would have had to accept that the first drink was an involuntary act, and also accept that alcoholism was a disease in the true sense of the word. In this case, the facts supported these contentions, but whether the argument would have been powerful enough for this particular judge, will never be known.

Case 10

A case involving intoxication with alcohol, but not related to driving, was that involving Mr. NF. One summer evening in 1987 NF, age 19, accompanied by three friends arrived at a local bar between 9:00 and 9:30 P.M. They remained at this establishment until 2:00 A.M., and while there consumed a quantity of alcohol, mainly in the form of beer. After leaving the bar, they all proceeded to walk to a railroad underpass to look at some murals that had been painted on the wall. NF stated that he stopped to urinate from the top of a wall on which they were walking, and claimed that he put his hand into an opening of a tower and was electrocuted. He had managed to pull his hand away and then fell through the tower floor to the ground.

Following the accident, he was admitted to the University Hospital, and the medical record from there indicated that he was admitted to the emergency room at 6:10 A.M., when a sample of his blood was taken and indicated a blood alcohol level of .043%. The accident had taken place at 5:45 A.M. at the time a power interruption from Suburban Station had been reported. This interruption of power is believed to have been caused by NF's contact with a live wire. It could therefore be stated that at the time of the accident, NF had a blood alcohol level of approximately .04%.

It is known that NF had been drinking beer on a regular basis since he was sixteen and in the eleventh grade. He consumed a six-pack of beer every other weekend and frequented bars since his freshman year in college. By August 30, 1987, he was therefore quite an experienced drinker who had consumed alcohol on a regular basis for at least three years prior to this accident. A blood alcohol level of .04% represents approximately two drinks containing either 12 oz of beer or one oz of 86-proof alcohol. NF was certainly a reasonably experienced drinker of alcohol who would have developed some tolerance to alcohol, as a result of his regular drinking since age sixteen. At the time of the accident, he weighed approximately 145 lbs and he would have reached a blood alcohol level of approximately .043% with the consumption of two 12-oz beers over a period of about one hour. In a person with even limited tolerance to alcohol, this blood alcohol level of .043% would not produce any easily observable signs or symptoms of alcohol intoxication. An opinion was given, with a reasonable degree of medical certainty that this level of alcohol in NF's blood played no substantial role in causing or contributing to the accident.

Although this was not a Dram Shop Act case, the bar could have been held liable for injuries sustained by NF if alcohol had been shown to be a substantial factor in the accident.

Case 11

A case which illustrates the complex relationships between alcohol intoxication, alcohol dependence and aggressive behavior was that of Mr. RA. This patient was evaluated by the author in May, 1994 and presented a history of having driven from workplace to a friend's house in April, 1992, arriving between 7:30 and 8:00 P.M. He had eaten lunch that day but had not eaten for at least six hours before arriving at his friend's home. Between 7:30 P.M. and 10:00 P.M. that evening, he consumed approximately six, 12-oz. bottles of beer and five shots of whiskey. He then drove with several of his friends to a bar and has only vague memories of this drive, which should have taken approximately five minutes. He recalled feeling "fuzzy" and driving "very carefully."

He arrived at the bar at approximately 10:30 P.M. and recalls going to the bathroom and then sitting in a booth with his friends, continuing to drink alcohol. They were all consuming beer and shots of whiskey and he remembered drinking at least five, 12-oz. beers and five shots between 10:30 P.M. and 1:30 A.M. He remembered being boisterous, speaking in a loud voice and laughing loudly. He also remembered indulging in what he described as "horseplay" and recalled laughing loudly, "joking around" and stumbling. His memories of that night were admittedly cloudy, but he described feeling as though he were "tuning out" and being "in a fog."

Around 1:30 in the morning, he recalled being involved in a fight and getting punched in the nose, but he was unsure by whom. He remembered a nosebleed and being thrown out of the bar by the bouncers. He recalled leaving the bar, walking to his car and then realizing that his friends were not with him. He felt concerned that there would be further violence and took a knife from his car before going back to look for his friends. He remembered being able to walk a distance to his car—approximately seventy-five feet—and then being on his way back, when he heard a lot of yelling, and then recalled that "all hell broke loose."

He described seeing men run towards him and told them that he had a knife, hoping that this would prevent further fighting. At this point, his memory became even more confused, but unfortunately a fight did result, during which he remembers being hit and falling to the ground. He has vague recollections of swinging his knife, running away from the scene and being hit by a car. Shortly after, he ran into the bar where police arrested him and took him to the police station. He was arrested, managed to make bail and was released, but at his trial ten months later he was sentenced to twenty-five months to five years in jail. He had been released just prior to his evaluation.

The patient's past history appeared to have been quite unremarkable, and he described himself as having been generally popular and able to sustain good relationships with friends and family. There was no history of any behavioral problems in his childhood or adolescence; schooling went well with no trouble in graduating from high school. He appears to have been of at least average intelligence and enjoyed himself in various sporting activities throughout his school years.

He first tasted alcohol at the age of fourteen when he drank some beer, and by the time he was fifteen years old he and his friends used to drink some beer on weekends. As he progressed through adolescence, he would continue to drink beer on weekends but never consumed more than two or three bottles. There was never dependence on alcohol, and he appears to have been well within the norm for his group so far as alcohol consumption was concerned. After leaving high school, he continued to drink beer as well as occasional spirits on weekends and rarely drank during the week. His only alcohol problem was an arrest in 1990 for driving under the influence and being put into an ARD program.

There was absolutely no history in this patient of any predisposition for violence or aggression. His childhood and adolescence were within normal limits, and he played the usual sports in school with no evidence of being prone to act out in an aggressive manner.

He was never written up or reported in high school for any antisocial activity and certainly never for any form of aggression. Since leaving high school, his behavior had also been characterized as being well controlled, and he does not seem to have had a particularly short temper or to have demonstrated any difficulties with impulse control. He had never been an initiator of any fights or altercations. Other than his arrest for driving under the influence of alcohol, he had no contact with the law prior to the incident which led to his arrest and, ultimately, imprisonment. While in prison, his behavior was exemplary, and there were no incidents of violence or fighting. He appears to have been a model prisoner, taking advantage of whatever educational opportunities that were offered, and spending his time working as productively as possible.

It was established that in April, 1992, at the time of the incident, RA was 6'1" tall and weighed 195 lbs. Between 7:30 P.M. and 10:30 P.M. he consumed approximately six, 12-oz. cans of beer and five shots of whiskey. Therefore, when he entered the bar, his blood alcohol concentration was approximately .15%. At this blood alcohol level, he was already in a state of considerable intoxication, and would have been poorly inhibited, unsteady on his feet and poorly coordinated. His vague memories of his drive to the bar are consistent with his blood alcohol level rising to .15%, and he would have had difficulty with his speech, slurring his words and some degree of boisterousness. While a patron at the bar between 10:30 P.M. and 1:30 A.M., he had consumed an additional five beers and five whiskeys, which would have resulted in his blood alcohol concentration rising from .15% to about .26% at 1:30 A.M. on the morning of the incident.

RA's recall of the events that occurred that night was consistent with someone who drank sufficient alcohol to become intoxicated and eventually arrive at a blood alcohol level of approximately .26%. He recalled feeling "hazy" and to have had a patchy memory of the events that occurred from the time he left his friend's house until he was ejected from the bar. This type of recall is characteristic of someone who is becoming intoxicated with alcohol, but it is perfectly reasonable to suppose that he would have had a recollection of the approximate quantity of alcohol that he consumed, as well as memories of many of the behaviors that he demonstrated. He does recall being boisterous, uninhibited and unsteady on his feet, and in a state of obvious intoxication with alcohol. He reported to the examiner that he was more intoxicated on that occasion than he had ever been in the past.

As he continued to consume alcohol at the bar, his blood alcohol level would have risen from .15%, and as it did so he would have demonstrated increasing signs of alcohol intoxication. As he is an individual with limited tolerance to alcohol, one would expect, in addition to an increase in a state of disinhibition, the presence of more boisterous behavior, loud speech, slurring of words, and more pronounced muscular incoordination, leading to an increase in the unsteady gait. It was pointed out that the great majority of individuals with a blood alcohol concentration rising from .15% to .26% would have demonstrated visible signs of intoxication.

It was the opinion of the expert, within a reasonable degree of medical certainty, that anyone trained to identify intoxicated individuals should have recognized the visible signs of intoxication in this individual while he was a patron at the bar. For the purposes of this particular case, it was also stated that another characteristic of being intoxicated with alcohol at this level would be such loss of inhibitory control that a person would be likely to respond more aggressively to real or imagined slights than he would when he was sober.

Release of aggressive behavior in fights is very common in people with blood alcohol levels as high as .26%. An opinion was offered that RA was affected with alcohol that night to an extent that there was a release of markedly aggressive behavior that was the direct cause of his being involved in the fight. His lack of inhibitory control was the proximate factor in causing him to use his knife in the way that was most uncharacteristic of this man. And it was the opinion of the author that, without alcohol in his system, he would not have manifested the behavior described.

When observed by the police following the fight, he did not appear to be in a state of obvious intoxication. The probable reason for this was that there was sufficient release of adrenaline as a result of the events that occurred, and, consequently, that he was capable of "pulling himself together" and acting in a reasonably sober manner in spite of still being intoxicated. The complex ramifications of this case are obvious and, since there are no rights or wrongs in this type of situation, the various potential outcomes should be weighed by the readers as though they were members of a jury considering this case.

9

DSM-IV, SUBSTANCE-RELATED DISORDERS, AND FORENSIC PSYCHIATRY

In the Fourth Edition of the American Psychiatric Association's *Diagnostic Statistical Manual of Mental Disorders,* or DSM-IV (17), alcohol-related disorders are found in the category designated as Substance-Related Disorders. The substances described have been grouped into eleven classes consisting of alcohol, amphetamines or similarly acting sympathomimetics, caffeine, cannabis, cocaine, hallucinogens, inhalants, nicotine, opioids, phencyclidine (PCP), and sedatives, hypnotics and anxiolytics. Pharmacologically, alcohol shares many features with the sedatives, hypnotics and anxiolytics, while cocaine shares features with amphetamines or similarly acting sympathomimetics. Included in this section are also Polysubstance Dependence and Other or Unknown Substance-Related Disorders.

Substance-Related Disorders can also be caused by many prescribed and over-the-counter medications. In these cases, symptoms are frequently related to the dosage of the medication and usually disappear when the dosage is lowered or the medication stopped. Idiosyncratic reactions have been observed to a single dose of some medications. Included in those medications that can cause substance-related disorders are anesthetics and analgesics, anticholinergic agents, anticonvulsants, antihistamines, antiparkinsonian medications, chemotherapeutic agents, corticosteroids, gastrointestinal medications, muscle relaxants, nonsteroidal anti-inflammatory medications, other over-the-counter medications, antidepressant medications and Antabuse. Toxic substances that may cause these disorders include heavy metals, such as lead or aluminum, rat poisons containing strychnine, pesticides containing acetylcholinesterase inhibitors, nerve gases, ethylene glycol (antifreeze), carbon monoxide, and carbon dioxide. Inhalants, such as fuel and paint are becoming increasingly common substances of abuse (huffing).

The substance-related disorders are divided into two groups:

1) the substance use disorders (substance dependence and substance abuse);

2) the substance-induced disorders (substance intoxication, substance withdrawal, substance-induced persisting amnestic disorder, substance-induced psychotic disorder, substance-induced mood disorder, substance-induced anxiety disorder, substance-induced sexual dysfunction and substance-induced sleep disorder).

SUBSTANCE DEPENDENCE

A diagnosis of substance dependence can be applied to every class of substances except caffeine. The essential feature of substance dependence is defined in DSM-IV as a "cluster of cognitive, behavioral, and physiological symptoms indicating that the individual continues use of the substance despite significant substance-related problems." Repeated exposure to the substance usually results in tolerance, withdrawal, and compulsive substance-taking behavior. An overwhelming subjective drive to use the substance (craving) is likely to be experienced by most individuals with substance dependence.

Dependence is characterized by tolerance, a withdrawal syndrome and continued use in spite of known psychological or physical problems caused by the drug.

Tolerance is the need for greatly increased amounts of the substance to achieve intoxication, or a markedly diminished effect with continued use of the same amount of the substance. The degree of tolerance varies greatly depending on the substances that are used. For example, use of opioids and stimulants usually result in substantial tolerance, while tolerance to alcohol could also be pronounced but usually much less so than for amphetamines. Tolerance has been demonstrated in animal studies and in some individuals for cannabis, but it is uncertain whether it develops at all to phencyclidine. The causes and types of tolerance are discussed in more detail elsewhere in this book.

Withdrawal is also discussed in more detail elsewhere, and is defined in DSM-IV as "a maladaptive behavioral change, with physiological and cognitive concomitants, that occurs when blood or tissue concentrations of the substance decline in an individual who had maintained prolonged heavy use of the substance." As a result of the development of withdrawal symptoms, the individual is more likely to take the substance to relieve or avoid those symptoms, and typically uses the substance from the time of wakening throughout the day. As with tolerance, withdrawal symptoms also vary greatly across the various classes of substances. Withdrawal symptoms are frequently seen with alcohol, opioids, sedatives, hypnotics and anxiolytics. These symptoms and signs are less apparent with drugs such as amphetamines and cocaine, while no withdrawal symptoms have been observed after the repeated use of hallucinogens or phencyclidine.

It must be noted that neither tolerance nor withdrawal is necessary, or in themselves sufficient, for a diagnosis of substance dependence. Specification as to "with physiological dependence" and to "without physiological dependence" is indicative of the presence or absence of tolerance or withdrawal.

SUBSTANCE ABUSE

Substance abuse is more likely to be seen in individuals who have only recently started taking the substance, but some individuals continue to have "substance-related adverse consequences" over a very long period of time without ever developing evidence of substance dependence.

SUBSTANCE INTOXICATION

Substance intoxication is often associated with substance abuse or dependence, and diagnosis is usually evident from the history, physical examination and toxicological analysis of body fluids. Substance intoxication is characterized by disturbances in perception, wakefulness, attention, thinking, judgment, psychomotor behavior, and interpersonal behavior. The clinical picture varies markedly among individuals and is also strongly influenced by the particular substance that is present, the dose and time taken to con-sume it, the individual's tolerance, the time elapsed since the last dose, the expectations of the substance s effect, and the setting or environment in which the substance was taken. Acute intoxication, where the substance is taken for a relatively short time, may be quite different from chronic intoxication, where a drug is taken for a prolonged period. Different substances can produce identical symptoms, and often the diagnosis is complicated by several sub-stances having been taken. The maladaptive behavior often results in accidents, general medical complications, disruption in social and family relationships, vocational or financial difficulties or legal problems. It is important to remember that signs and symptoms of intoxication may sometimes persist for hours or days beyond the time when the substance was detectable in the body fluids. These long-term effects of intoxication need to be distinguished from sub-stance withdrawal, where the symptoms are initiated by a decline in blood or tissue concentrations of a substance.

SUBSTANCE WITHDRAWAL

Substance withdrawal is usually, but not always, associated with substance dependence. It is extremely common for individuals suffering from withdrawal to experience a craving to take the par-ticular substance again to reduce the withdrawal symptoms. A withdrawal syndrome is well recognized for alcohol, ampheta-mines, cocaine, nicotine, opioids, and sedatives, hypnotics and anxiolytics. Withdrawal symptoms vary according to the substance, with most symptoms being the opposite of those observed in in-toxication with the same substance. Withdrawal develops when doses are reduced or stopped, whereas signs and symptoms of in-toxication improve after dosing stops.

IMPLICATIONS FOR FORENSIC PSYCHIATRY IN THE USE OF DSM-IV

This latest and best attempt to classify psychiatric disorders in the United States still, of course, has several limitations. Many of these are discussed in detail in the *Manual*, and some are specific to the use of DSM-IV in forensic settings.

One of the main objectives of DSM-IV is to provide a common language for professionals in the mental health and allied fields; it was developed "for use in clinical, educational, and research settings," and is intended to be utilized by appropriately trained and experienced individuals. *The Diagnostic and Statistical Manual of Mental Disorders* should not be thought of as a "cookbook, "nor should the lists of specific diagnostic criteria take the place of sophisticated clinical judgment. Clinical judgment remains the hallmark of psychiatric diagnosis, and this fact needs to be strongly emphasized by the forensic expert presenting testimony in court.

DSM-IV is a categorical system of classification (as opposed to a dimensional model) in which mental disorders are divided according to sets of criteria. A dimensional system is based on quantification of attributes, rather than assignment to categories. Identification of disease categories has long been the traditional system in medical diagnosis and works optimally when diagnostic classes are homogeneous, when the various classes have clear boundaries and when the classes are mutually exclusive. Limitations in these regards are present in general medical classification, but are particularly thorny issues in clinical psychiatry.

Categories of mental disorder as defined in DSM-IV are not totally discreet entities with unconditional boundaries separating them from no mental disorder, or other mental disorders. Also, and especially important for forensic psychiatry, those individuals included in the same category of mental disorder differ from one another in many significant ways. This diversity creates a significant number of "boundary" cases, and, consequently, it is always necessary to record and present as much clinical information as possible, in addition to the "DSM-IV diagnosis." The *Manual* has responded in part to this dissimilarity in clinical cases by including sets of criteria from which subsets of items from a longer list will qualify an individual for that diagnosis.

In forensic settings, one cannot overemphasize the fact that the specific diagnostic criteria found *in The Diagnostic and Statistical Manual of Mental Disorders* were intended to be viewed as simply "guidelines" for clinical diagnosis and *not* for forensic purposes. The presence of sufficient criteria to allow for a *clinical* diagnosis would not necessarily satisfy the *legal* requirements for the existence of "mental defect," "mental disability," or "mental disorder." A diagnosis based on DSM-IV criteria alone will usually not be sufficient to establish competence, criminal responsibility or disability. In these kinds of situations, we are more concerned about what "impairments" an individual has, and how these affect the particular abilities we are considering. DSM-IV diagnoses do not imply any specific level of disability or impairment, and therefore have a limited application in most legal settings.

Other issues in forensic settings, that are of even more significance than in most clinical settings, are the degree of control that an individual has over his or her behavior, and the etiology of the mental disorder. The etiology, or cause, of psychiatric diseases is very poorly understood, and is most likely biopsychosocial. Thus, inclusion of a mental disorder in DSM-IV is not contingent on any knowledge of its etiologic factors. The diagnosis, reads the DSM-IV, "does not carry any necessary implications regarding the causes of the individual's mental disorder or of its associated impairments," and "does not carry any necessary implications regarding the individual's degree of control over the behaviors that may be associated with the disorder."

These caveats aside, DSM-IV is an essential text for the forensic psychiatrist. Used appropriately, it is of great value in supporting a diagnosis of psychiatric disease and is a classification system that is accepted by the vast majority of practicing psychiatrists. The objective nature of the criteria as presented in DSM-IV, and their relevance to the existence of a mental disorder, are invaluable in allowing forensic experts to communicate in an easily understood fashion with judges, attorneys and jurors.

10

LANDMARK INTOXICATION CASES

THE BREATHALYZER TEST: *STATE V. DOWNIE*

This appeal (56) involved yet another challenge to the scientific reliability of Breathalyzers. Specifically, defendants challenged the accuracy of the Breathalyzer test results based on partition-ratio variability.

Defendants were charged with violating a law which makes it unlawful for a person to operate "a motor vehicle with a blood alcohol concentration of 0.10% or more etc. in the defendant's blood...." This provision enacted by 1983 amendment defines the per se violation of driving while intoxicated ("DWI"). The Breathalyzer, the machine the State employs is to ascertain blood alcohol, measures the amount of alcohol in the breath and multiplies that by 2100 to arrive at the level of alcohol in the arterial blood supplying alcohol to the brain. This 2100:1 partition ratio presumes that every 2.1 liters (2100 milliliters) of expired alveolar air (or air expired in the last 1/3 portion of a deep breath) contains approximately the same quantity of alcohol as one milliliter of blood. If a person's actual blood-breath ratio is lower than 2100:1, the Breathalyzer will overestimate blood alcohol, and vice-versa.

Defendants asserted that because people have broadly divergent ratios of breath alcohol relative to blood alcohol, the 2100:1 partition ratio is inaccurate and the Breathalyzer-test results premised on that partition ratio are scientifically unreliable.

Downie sought a pretrial hearing in order to present expert testimony regarding the scientific unreliability of Breathalyzer-test results. To economize on the costs of presenting that testimony, Downie moved to consolidate his case with the drunk-driving cases of three other defendants also represented by his attorney. The cases arose in four different municipalities, all served by the same municipal court judge, who consolidated the four actions with regard to common questions of law and fact and granted a pre-trial conference.

The experts who testified before the trial court were Drs. Borkenstein, Hlastaia, Payne, Jones, Dubowski, and Simpson, Messrs. Shajani, Lucas, and Harding, and Sgt. Cullberg. Dr. Borkenstein, who invented the Breathalyzer commented on its scientific reliability. Dr. Hlastaia outlined potential physical variables that could affect the blood-breath experimental studies. Messrs. Shajani and Lucas, Harding and Sgt. Cullburg explored their own field work and laboratory studies. Dr. Simpson analyzed the works of others from a statistical perspective, but presented no experimental or field work of his own.

After hearing the experts' interpretation of the physiological data, the lower court found the seven following conclusions of fact.

1) The Breathalyzer, Models 900 and 900A, is a scientifically reliable and accurate device for measurement of the alcohol content of a person's breath (assuming proper functioning of the instrument and a qualified operator).

2) In converting at a ratio of 1 to 2100 the breath-alcohol concentration present in the person's blood, the Breathalyzer reading is not scientifically accurate.

3) Calculated blood-breath ratios are worthless for forensic purposes. They are subject to so many variables as to be unusable except for gross estimates of a person's true lung partition ratio, and then only at a particular moment. (Borkenstein, Dubowski, Payne, Jones, Lucas).

4) In a prosecution for drunk driving, the Breathalyzer calibrated at 2100 to 1 is biased in favor of the accused: a) It under-reads the average person's blood alcohol by some 9% or 10%, compared to a venous whole-blood sample that might be simultaneously taken; b) Its truncated readings give the accused the benefit of anywhere from .001% to .009% on a given test reading; c) The start line

set on the Breathalyzer scale gives the subject the benefit of another .003% on any test reading. (All experts agree on the foregoing.); d) The lower value of two consecutive readings taken fifteen minutes apart is used for proof.

5) The Breathalyzer gives a correct reading of alcohol in the breath at a particular moment. It does not distinguish between pre-peak "absorptive" stages in the intake and elimination of alcohol in the blood. Those terms are of value only to the scientist.

6) The Breathalyzer does not overestimate alcohol in the blood at the .10% level to the detriment of the accused. That is clearly so in the post-peak stage. In the pre-peak stage the Breathalyzer reading is more accurate in predicting the amount of alcohol affecting the brain than is a venous blood sample and it cannot be empirically demonstrated that it is in error, so long as two breath readings are taken within fifteen minutes of each other, do not differ by more than .01%, and the lower of the two is used for proof purposes. (Jones, Shajani, Dubowski, Lucas).

7) For the Breathalyzer to give readings that can be used with confidence, the operator must be sure that at least twenty minutes have expired since the last ingestion of alcohol to avoid the presence of "mouth" alcohol, which can give a falsely high reading.

The Attorney General suggested that Conclusions of Finding 2 and 3 be expanded to read as follows:

The Breathalyzer is calibrated at a breath/blood conversion ratio of 1 to 2100 in determining the amount of alcohol in an individual's system. Use of a 1 to 2100 ratio in the conversion of measured breath alcohol concentration to venous blood alcohol concentration is scientifically inaccurate in that it results in an underestimation of venous blood alcohol concentration. The more scientifically acceptable conversion ratio is 1 to 2300. However, the forensic scientific community, aware that a 1 to 2100 ratio benefits a defendant, has retained this ratio for law enforcement purposes.

The Attorney General further suggested that the following sentences be added to Finding 3:

> For this reason, a comparison of the actual differences between breath test and venous blood test results is the only valid form of analysis of the accuracy of breath testing instruments calibrated at a 2100:1 ratio to determine venous blood alcohol concentration. Reliable empirical evidence demonstrates that these actual differences are very small.

Experts generally agreed on the physiological process triggered by the ingestion of alcohol A relatively small percentage of ethyl alcohol (the alcohol contained in alcoholic beverages) is absorbed directly through the stomach into the blood that carries it to the brain. The remaining alcohol is absorbed through the intestinal tract. The alcohol reaches the brain via the carotid arteries. The amount of alcohol present in the water in the brain is what affects the driver's ability to operate a motor vehicle. After passing through the brain, the blood travels back through the venous system to the liver, the heart and back into the arterial system and lungs. The liver metabolizes the alcohol. Once absorbed, the alcohol will continue to affect the brain until it is completely metabolized.

The body undergoes at least two metabolic phases following the ingestion of alcohol. The absorptive (pre-peak) phase lasts from the initial ingestion of an alcoholic drink to the point of the peak-alcohol blood level. The rate of absorption depends on variables, such as the amount of food in the stomach, the amount of pure alcohol ingested, and the rate of drinking. That initial phase is followed by the post-absorptive (post-peak) phase, which witnesses a decline in alcohol-blood levels.

During the post-absorptive phase, most experts agree that venous blood, arterial blood, and breath are all good indicators of the amount of alcohol in the brain. During the absorptive phase, however, arterial blood, which takes the alcohol to the brain, is the most accurate measure of alcohol in the brain. Venous blood may underestimate the amount of alcohol in the brain during the absorptive period because it does not circulate close to the brain and is entirely dependent on the amount of alcohol derived from the intestines. Thus, during the absorption period arterial blood may reflect a much higher percentage of alcohol than venous blood.

Ideally, arterial blood, drawn from the carotid artery, would furnish the most accurate estimate of alcohol in the brain. Yet, a complicated, painful, and potentially dangerous procedure is necessary to draw arterial blood. The arterial blood does carry the alcohol to the lungs where it diffuses into the alveolar air space and is exhaled in the breath. Because of that, many experts consider alveolar air, or air expelled from the lungs at the end of a deep breath, as the best practical measure of alcohol in the brain during the absorptive phase. Capillary blood, drawn from the fingertip and emanating from the shunt between the arterial and venous systems, is also a sound measurement of alcohol during the absorptive phase.

For law enforcement purposes, the drawing of capillary blood and venous blood are a more intrusive and burdensome test than the Breathalyzer. They require puncturing the body of a suspected drunk driver by experienced medical personnel who can and must take meticulous care that blood samples not become contaminated. Capillary blood drawn from the fingertip is small in amount and the alcohol it contains easily evaporates when exposed to the air. Extraction of venous blood, while not posing a problem with evaporation, is an invasive procedure requiring trained medical personnel. Moreover, venous blood is unreliable in reading the amount of alcohol affecting the brain during the absorptive phase.

In contrast, the Breathalyzer may be administered by a trained police officer, and requires only that the suspect exhale deeply into the machine. Assuming the machine is in working order, and the test is properly administered, all experts agree the Breathalyzer can read the amount of alcohol in the breath with a great deal of accuracy. The operative inquiry is then whether the Breathalyzer may overestimate blood alcohol to the extent that some drivers would be erroneously convicted.

The Breathalyzer applies Henry's law to the blood which courses through the lungs carrying alcohol. As the arterial blood passes through the lungs, some of the alcohol will become vaporized in the alveolar air and expelled in the breath. The Breathalyzer is calibrated to presume that at 34° Celsius, a solution of .121 grams of alcohol per 100 milliliters of water will give off alcohol to the vapor of .10 grams per 210 liters of vapor. Thus, we arrive at the current 2100:1 partition ratio. A person's partition ratio may vary from time to time. Moreover, it may be that no two people have the exact same partition ration. Thus, the 2100:1 partition ratio is merely an estimate that roughly approximates most people's ratio and that is calibrated to give the benefit of the doubt to the subject in most instances.

Expert witnesses generally agreed that the Breathalyzer,, using a 2100:1 partition ratio, will usually underestimate the amount of alcohol in the blood and these, among other less-significant factors, cause the Breathalyzer to render many more results on the low side than on the high side.

Dr. Borkenstein testified that a 2300:1 partition ratio would probably result in more accurate Breathalyzer readings. He estimated that 9% of Breathalyzer readings indicate a lower amount of alcohol in the blood than blood-test readings would indicate. In contrast, he estimated that only three persons in a thousand might be convicted as a result of an erroneously-high Breathalyzer reading. He adduced that Breathalyzer researchers and members of the National Safety Council adopted the 2100:1 partition ratio instead of the more accurate 2300:1 ratio because they wanted to err on the low side and have almost no errors on the high side.

Despite the evidence that the Breathalyzer could potentially wrongfully convict less than 2.4% of suspected drunk drivers, some scientists still pose objections to the test based on the infinite physical factors that affect the blood-breath ratio. Biological factors, such as mouth temperature, gender, body temperature, medication, menstrual cycle, and oral contraceptives may have some theoretical effect on Breathalyzer readings. In addition, hematocrit, or the ratio of the volume of blood cells to the total volume of blood, expressed as a percentage, may have some theoretical effect. Women have generally lower hematocrit meaning a lower percentage of their blood is comprised of cells, and therefore a higher percentage is comprised of water. No scientist during the remand hearing could establish that these theoretical effects were sufficiently concrete as to be significant. Moreover, these factors would not always inflate Breathalyzer readings. Even defense witnesses admitted that some of these factors would actually lower Breathalyzer readings.

The review of the record on remand was in conformity with the conclusion of fact determined by the trial court. The conclusion was that the Breathalyzer is a reliable and indispensable tool for law enforcement purposes.

It is important to note the legislature's statutory pronouncement on drunk driving. N.J.S.A. 39:4-50(a) states that "[a] person who operates a motor vehicle with a blood alcohol concentration of 0.10% or more by weight of alcohol in the defendant's blood" is guilty and subject to punishment. N.J.S.A. 39:4-50.2 states that drivers on public roads consent to the taking of breath samples for the purpose of ascertaining their blood-alcohol levels (provided the test is administered according to statutory standards). Finally, N.J.S.A. 39:4-50.3 provides that the Attorney General has the authority to promulgate breath-testing procedures and standards governing the qualification and competence of those who administer the test.

Others who testified before the Senate Committee echoed the Attorney General's reliance on the Breathalyzer. The Director of the Division of Motor Vehicles spoke of scientific testing as being definitive of the individual's level of impairment. The President of the New Jersey Licensed Beverage Association referred to "the approximate number of cocktails one would need to consume" so that "the scientific reading to discover the alcohol content would be .10%." The then-Superintendent of the State Police summarized the tenor of the hearings when he stated that the chemical test, or "drunkometer" (analogous to our present Breathalyzer), "is the best method of separating the innocent from the guilty." Although chemical tests may refer to a broader class than just the Breathalyzer, comments regarding the reliability of the Breathalyzer pervaded the hearings. There was an assumption underlying the hearings that a Breathalyzer reading of .10% should be sufficient to establish impairment.

In conclusion, the Breathalyzer fulfills legislative policy and intent to provide a reliable and fair measure of alcohol in the brain. Breathalyzer results can continue to be used in prosecution of the per se offense of drunk driving. The reliability of Breathalyzer results will continue to be the subject of judicial notice in drunk-driving prosecutions. Extrapolation evidence will also continue to be admissible.

The Breathalyzer is unsurpassed in its combined practicality and usefulness. It errs on the low side in a significant number of cases, in order not to overestimate blood alcohol in the greatest possible number of cases.

COMMENTARY

For those involved in the litigation of driving-while-intoxicated cases, *State v. Downie* has great significance. It clearly establishes the legitimacy of the Breathalyzer and gives the reader a full understanding of the theory behind the use of this instrument, and the role it plays in the field of drunk driving. It provides the information necessary to allow an expert to intelligently interact with the judicial system in cases where the Breathalyzer has been used, and to confidently support the validity of the blood alcohol concentrations obtained as a result of the use of this instrument.

ROBERTS V. PEOPLE (57)

DEFINITIONS

Voluntariness

The voluntary intoxication requirement has been interpreted to mean that "the intoxicant has been introduced into the actor's system with his knowledge and without force or fraud" (58). The Model Penal Code uses the term "self-induced" intoxication instead of "voluntary" intoxication and defines the term to mean "intoxication caused by substances which the actor knowingly introduces into his body, the tendency of which to cause intoxication he knows or ought to know, unless he introduces them pursuant to medical advice or under such circumstances as would afford a defense to a charge of crime."

Accordingly, voluntary intoxication "is not limited to those instances in which drunkenness was definitely desired or intended but includes all instances of culpable intoxication (58). Intoxication is, therefore, deemed voluntary even though the drinking was induced by the persuasion or the example of another. Moreover, merely because someone else provided the intoxicant does not necessarily render the resulting intoxication involuntary.

A variety of circumstances in which intoxication is considered to be acquired involuntarily have been recognized. Under one theory, intoxication is deemed to be involuntary "if it is the result of a genuine mistake as to the nature or character of the liquor or drug. ... or if it has resulted from taking something not known to be capable of producing such a result, as through the fraud or contrivance of another." Put another way, "intoxication is not voluntary if brought about by the fraud, artifice, or stratagem of another."

For example, in *State v. Alie* (59), an innocent victim unknowingly consumed "knock-out" drops supplied by another to help facilitate a robbery. In *People v. Penman* (60), an innocent victim unknowingly consumed cocaine tablets provided by a friend, who described the tablets as being "breath perfumers." In each case, the victim later committed a homicide while under the influence of the drug that was previously taken. In both instances the court found that the victim would be innocent of homicide if the claimed facts were true, as the slayings would have occurred as a result of involuntary intoxication.

Intoxication

In order to amount to intoxication in the legal sense, it is generally required that the consumption of intoxicants be such as "to create a state of mental confusion, excluding the possibility of specific intent." Thus, a defendant could be under the influence of an intoxicant and nonetheless not be intoxicated for purposes of negating a pertinent intent element of an offense.

Specific Intent - General Intent Crime

A crime may be labeled as a specific intent crime either by legislative prescription or through common-law interpretation. By one definition, specific intent is "a particular criminal intent beyond the act done." General intent has therefore been viewed as the minimum mens rea element present in every common-law crime.

Because the law holds one responsible for his actions, including criminal conduct, voluntary intoxication offers no hope for one accused of a general intent crime. In the case of a specific intent crime, the issue becomes one of degree, i.e., when is the accused sufficiently intoxicated to negate the specific intent element of the crime charged?

In *Roberts v. People* (57), the defendant was charged with assault with intent to commit murder. Roberts had argued with Charles E. Greble over a quantity of wood that the defendant agreed to provide. This dispute resulted in a confrontation in which the defendant drew a revolver and fired three rounds at Greble, missing on each attempt. Roberts was arrested and taken into custody where he slept until one o'clock the next afternoon. When he awoke he claimed no recollection of the preceding day's events, but indicated that he had consumed some quantity of alcohol prior to his memory failure.

At trial, the defendant presented evidence to show that a hereditary history of mental illness, coupled with the fact that use of intoxicating liquors tended to provoke insanity in his family, resulted in a loss of his mental faculties at the time of the alleged shooting, which was sufficient to absolve him of any criminal responsibility. The state rebutted by offering evidence to show that "the defendant was deprived of the use of his mental faculties at and before and after the assault by his own voluntary intoxication."

The trial court rejected the defendant's theory and charged the jury:

> Voluntary intoxication of the defendant at the time of the assault, will not excuse him.
>
> It is claimed by the defense, however, that although intoxication will not excuse the act of the party, it takes away the element of specific intent; that the assault was an innocent act, unless done with a corrupt or malicious motive
>
> In what sense could the assault with a deadly weapon be considered innocent? Does not the very act, with its circumstances, carry proof of intention which is irresistible?
>
> The power and direction which bore the respondent to the place where Greble was to be found, and identified him

there, and which aimed the pistol, fired it, and repeated the discharge, carried with it to other minds the inference of intention...

The defendant was convicted of the crime charged.

An appeal ensued.

On the issue of intoxication, the state argued that the court's earlier decision in *Carbutt* (61) controlled: Voluntary intoxication is no excuse for a crime. The issue before the *Roberts* court, however, was whether the defendant's claim of voluntary intoxication was a defense to the specific intent element of the crime charged.

The court first observed that had the defendant formed the criminal intent while sober, he would have possessed the requisite specific criminal intent prior to his intoxication and 'his subsequent voluntary intoxication would not shield him from a conviction...." Further, the *Roberts* court affirmed the earlier decision that one who places himself into a condition of voluntary intoxication must be held responsible for the consequence of his actions. The court distinguished the intent to commit a crime (specific intent) from the act committed (general intent) and viewed as relevant the inquiry as to whether the defendant, at the time of the alleged offense was incapable of entertaining the intent as charged.

To assess such capacity, the court considered several factors:

1) the nature and circumstances of the assault;

2) the actions, conduct, and demeanor of the accused;

3) declarations made by the accused at the time of the alleged crime and thereafter; and

4) how far the mental faculties must be obscured by intoxication to render the accused incapable of entertaining the intent charged.

Although the fourth factor appears to beg the question of intent, the court focused on that issue to distinguish the required level of mental awareness called for by differing criminal actions:

This last question involves another aspect of intent, such as that to defraud, when the result intended is more indirect and remote, or only to be brought about by a series or combination of causes and effects, would naturally involve a greater number of ideas, and require a more complicated mental process, than the simple intent to kill by the discharge of a loaded pistol. The question we are now considering related solely to the capacity of the defendant to entertain this particular intent. It is a question rather of the exercise of the will than of reasoning powers.

"In determining the question whether the assault was committed with the intent charged, it was therefore material to inquire whether the defendant's mental faculties were so far overcome by the effect of intoxication, as to render him incapable of entertaining the intent." The court then shifted to the trial court's intoxication instruction and, finding it in error, offered the following as a matter of law:

> "I think the jury should have been instructed, that if his mental faculties were so far overcome by the intoxication, that he was not conscious of what he was doing, or if he did know what he was doing, but did not know why he was doing it, or that his actions and the means he was using were naturally adapted or calculated to endanger life or produce death; then he had not sufficient capacity to entertain the intent, and in that event they could not infer that intent from his acts...."

This passage is referred to as the "capacity standard" because it focuses not on the actual intent held by the actor, but rather upon the ability of the accused to entertain a specific criminal intent. Consequently, use of this test might be viewed as an indirect approach because the jury is initially diverted from the issue of actual intent to determine the defendant's capacity to entertain such intent. If the defendant lacks sufficient capacity, the absence of actual intent is presumed—much like an irrebuttable presumption in strict liability tort law. Once certain elements are found to be present, such as intoxication sufficient to render one incapable of forming the specific intent charged, the issue of actual intent is not addressed nor can it be inferred from the acts of the accused.

COMMENTARY

Since its decision in *Roberts v. People,* the Michigan Supreme Court has recognized voluntary intoxication as a defense only to specific intent crimes. Intoxication due to the fault of another, accident, inadvertence, or mistake of the consumer, or by some physical or psychological dependence (i.e., involuntary) is a complete defense, although this is by no means universally accepted. For example, some courts have held that a person who voluntarily drinks but unwittingly consumes added intoxicants is nonetheless barred from claiming involuntary intoxication as a defense. There is jurisdictional variability for this and similar claims.

A criminal act committed during delirium tremens can be defended on the basis that the perpetrator was unable to realize the quality of his or her act, was unable to distinguish right from wrong. The mental and physiological symptoms present in delirium tremens are interpreted in a similar manner to being in a state of insanity. It is thus a complete defense provided the accused is not intoxicated when the criminal act is committed. Evidence of intoxication is fatal to a delirium tremens defense, and the accused must then prove the lack of requisite capacity under *Roberts* which has been applied for over one hundred years.

For a more in-depth discussion of the ramifications of an intoxication defense, the reader is recommended to read "Voluntary Intoxication: A Defense to Specific Intent Crimes" (62).

As discussed elsewhere, this area is of great complexity and uncertainty with confusion persisting in spite of repeated attempts to clarify the law. The following three cases illustrate some of the problems encountered, and will help the reader to appreciate the very real difficulties that develop in the litigation of cases involving intoxication.

"INTOXICATION," JURY INSTRUCTIONS:
COMMONWEALTH OF PENNSYLVANIA V. RANDY JOE REIFF (63)

Defendant was convicted by jury in the Court of Common Pleas, Crawford County, Criminal Division, Meadville, Pennsylvania, 1978, of first-degree murder and other offenses. Defendant appealed. The Supreme Court, No. 179 March Term, 1979, held that evidence did not require giving an instruction on effect of intoxication on capability of forming specific intent.

"Drinking" and "intoxication" are not synonymous terms, and mere evidence of drinking did not require instruction, in prosecution for homicide and other offenses, on the effect of intoxication upon capability of forming specific intent.

OPINION OF THE COURT

LARSEN, Justice.

Appellant, Randy Joe Reiff, was convicted by a jury of murder of the first degree, unlawful restraint, and terrorist threats. The convictions arose from the fatal shooting of Douglas Castle in Meadville Pennsylvania, on August 14, 1979. Following the denial of post-trial motions, appellant was sentenced to a term of life imprisonment on the murder of the first degree charge and to a concurrent term of two and one-half to five years imprisonment on the remaining charges.

Appellant first contends that the lower court erred in refusing his requested instruction on the defense of voluntary intoxication. Section 308 of the Crimes Code states:

"Neither voluntary intoxication nor involuntary drugged condition is a defense to a criminal charge, nor may evidence of such [intoxication] be introduced to negative the element of intent of the offense, except that evidence of such intoxication or drugged condition of the defendant may be offered by the defendant whenever it is relevant to reduce murder from a higher degree to a lower degree of murder."

Appellant alleges that sufficient evidence was introduced at trial to establish that he was "intoxicated" at the time of the shooting and, therefore, incapable of forming the specific intent necessary to commit murder of the first degree. Appellant did not testify at trial. However, a statement given by appellant to police following his arrest was read into the record at trial. In this statement, appellant related that he smoked "some" marijuana more than four hours before the shooting occurred and that he may have drank four or five quarts of beer. Appellant made no reference to being intoxicated on the night of the shooting and his recollection of the evening's events was lucid.

The testimony at trial established that appellant and a friend, Donald Buchanan, were at Kacy's Saloon in Meadville from approximately 9:30 P.M. until 1:00 A.M. on the night of the shooting. This testimony (Buchanan and Richie Cady, the bartender) showed that appellant drank approximately two and one-half quarts of beer during this period of time. This testimony further revealed that appellant exhibited no signs of intoxication and that there was nothing unusual about appellant's behavior. Furthermore, there was no evidence that appellant ingested any intoxicants after leaving Kacy's Saloon.

The key word in the voluntary intoxication statute is "intoxication." "Intoxication" is a non-technical word which Webster's Dictionary (unabridged 2nd ed., 1976) defines as a "making or becoming drunk." "Drunk" is defined by Webster's Dictionary as "overwhelmed or overpowered by alcoholic liquor to the point of losing control over one's faculties." Drinking and intoxication are not synonymous terms; therefore a jury instruction on intoxication is not warranted because evidence of drinking is introduced at trial. It is the intention of the legislature that a defendant be overwhelmed or overpowered by alcoholic liquor to the point of losing his or her faculties or sensibilities before an intoxication instruction be given.

In the instant case, there was no evidence that appellant was intoxicated or had lost his faculties or sensibilities. *In Commonwealth v. Kichline* (64), this court stated that there must be sufficient evidence of intoxication in the record to bring that issue into the case before the trial court is required to instruct the jury on an intoxication defense. As there was insufficient evidence of intoxication in the record, the trial court did not err in refusing to instruct the jury on an intoxication defense.

The testimony at trial revealed that, for several weeks prior to the slaying, appellant had been dating one Linda Bly. After leaving Kacy's Saloon early in the morning of August 14, 1978 (date of the slaying), appellant went to Linda Bly's apartment, and learned from a baby-sitter that Linda was across the hall in Douglas Castle's (victim's) apartment. Upon finding the door to the victim's apartment unlocked, appellant entered the apartment and discovered Linda in bed with the victim. Appellant announced, while brandishing a gun, "I'm going to blow you away." The victim told appellant to leave the apartment, to which appellant responded, "It's not for you to say " I'm the one with the gun." The victim them attempted to get out of bed but, as he stepped over Linda, he tripped and fell forward, striking appellant s gun hand. Appellant retreated two steps and fired the gun once, striking the victim in the neck.

Justice Roberts, concurring, stated: "I agree with the majority that the judgment of sentence should be affirmed. I cannot, however, subscribe to the majority's analysis of appellant's "intoxication" claim. Despite the bold assertion of the majority, there is no evidence that our Legislature intends "that a defendant be overwhelmed or overpowered by alcoholic liquor to the point of losing his or her faculties or sensibilities before an intoxication instruction be given." Rather, there need exist only a reasonable doubt as to a defendant's sobriety at the time of the offense to justify an intoxication instruction. In my view, there is no evidence here creating such a doubt. The trial court thus properly declined to instruct the jury on intoxication."

ALCOHOL AND SPECIFIC INTENT: FIRST DEGREE MURDER
COMMONWEALTH OF PENNSYLVANIA V. ANTHONY LEE CESSNA (65)

Defendant pleaded guilty to general charge of murder and verdict of guilty of murder in the first degree was entered by County, and defendant appealed. The Superior Court, No. 131 Harrisburg 1987, Glazewski, J., held that evidence was sufficient to find requisite specific intent despite claimed use of LSD.

To negate intent necessary for conviction of murder in the first degree, a defendant must have been overwhelmed by drug to the point of losing his faculties so as to be incapable of forming a specific intent to kill. Evidence of a drugged condition as negating intent necessary for conviction of murder in the first degree is submitted for consideration of the fact finder, who may believe any, all, or none of the testimony offered at trial.

Evidence in first-degree murder prosecution was sufficient to contradict defendant's assertion that he was so drugged by use of

LSD at the time of shooting that he could not have formed requisite specific intent, and evidence was sufficient to establish that defendant shot his stepfather willfully, deliberately and with premeditation.

Appellant first challenges the sufficiency of the evidence to support the premeditation element of first-degree murder. Specifically, appellant contends that his voluntary ingestion of LSD prior to the murder negated the specific intent necessary to sustain a first-degree murder conviction. The appropriate test is whether the evidence of a drugged condition, if believed, may operate to negate the intent necessary for a conviction of murder in the first degree (66). A defendant, however, must have been so overwhelmed by the drug to the point of losing his faculties so as to be incapable of forming a specific intent to kill. The Supreme Court has declared that evidence of a drugged condition is submitted for consideration to the fact finder, who determines the validity of the claim. The trial of fact may believe any, all, or none of the testimony offered at trial (67).

In the instant case, regarding appellant's alleged ingestion of LSD, the appellant testified that he bought the LSD at an unidentified truck stop from someone he did not know. Additionally, appellant never mentioned his LSD experience until at least ten days after his arrest when appellant's prior counsel found marijuana in appellant's bedroom and asked him if he had taken drugs at the time of the shooting. Also, on the night of the shooting, appellant, while allegedly under the influence of LSD, found the keys to his stepfather's car, took the murder weapon and an extra set of clothes to a friend's house, and acted like "the same Tony [his friend] had always known."

The trial court, considering the foregoing, acted within its discretion as fact finder and discounted appellant's testimony of drug use and concluded on the basis of the remaining evidence that when appellant "fired the rifle at Richard Neidig's head, he did so with a specific intent to kill." We agree that there is sufficient evidence in the record to contradict appellant's assertion that he was so drugged at the time of the shooting that he could not have formed the requisite specific intent. We also agree that there was sufficient evidence to establish that appellant shot his stepfather willfully, deliberately, and with premeditation (68). As the Commonwealth's brief aptly sets forth:

> The Commonwealth presented testimony from Nannette Beahm, who was the [appellant's] girlfriend until the day of the shooting. The [appellant] had complained to her about his stepfather, that he didn't treat the [appellant] like a son and didn't love him. During the month before the shooting, the [appellant] told her about four times that he was going to "get a silencer gun and shoot him (Neidig) while he was sleeping and put him in his car and then go to a mountain and throw him in the side of a ditch in this mountain." The [appellant] asked her not to tell anyone of his plans. The Commonwealth also presented testimony from Cary Mull, who said that, two or three times during the month before the shooting, the [appellant] told Mull that he was going to "plug" his [step]father. In his statement [which was read to the court], the [appellant] said that he took his [step]dad's 30-06 rifle about two days before the shooting and hid it in his closet with the intention of shooting his [step]dad at a later time.

> He also said he had taken a live 30-06 bullet from the kitchen china closet. He waited until everyone was asleep, went to his [step]dad's room, and sat there with the gun for about ten minutes. He brought the gun up to shoot, but it did not go off because it was not cocked. He cocked the gun, put the barrel a foot to a foot-and-a-half from his [step]dad's head, and fired. He turned on the light and saw that the bullet had mangled the whole top of his dad's head.

> We are satisfied that the Commonwealth presented sufficient evidence to convict appellant of first-degree murder.

INTOXICATION INSTRUCTION: ASSAULT CASE:
UNITED STATES OF AMERICA V. LEIGHTON LEE FAY (69)

Defendant was convicted in the United States District Court for the District of South Dakota of assault resulting in serious bodily injury, assault with dangerous weapon, and of assault by striking, beating or wounding, and defendant appealed. The Court of Appeals, Henley, Circuit Judge, held that evidence warranted instruction as to intoxication and its effect upon defendant's intent.

The charges against defendant arose out of what was apparently a New Year's Day free-for-all involving defendant, an Indian male, and a number of Indian women. On December 31, 1980 defendant drove from Oglala, South Dakota, on the Pine Ridge Reservation to a New Year s Eve celebration at a bowling alley in Eagle Butte, South Dakota, on the Cheyenne-Eagle Butte Indian Reservation. He was accompanied by his girlfriend Agnes Randall, her aunt Verna Flying Hawk, and her cousin Fay Charging Thunder. They were later joined at the bowling alley by Leah Black Moon. At some point during the festivities, Leah became engaged in an altercation with Sylvia High Bear. One of Sylvia's companions, Anita Traversie, was knocked from her stool, and it appears that Fay, Agnes, and possibly Verna also became involved. Both groups were asked to leave sometime after midnight.

The record reveals as many different accounts of the subsequent events as there were witnesses. It appears, however, that defendant went with Agnes, Fay, Verna, and Leah to Leah's home, and that later in the morning, Sylvia's sister Freda Fish came to Leah's house accompanied by Sylvia's daughter Pauline High Bear, and Anita. It is not clear how the women got inside the house, but once they were inside several fights ensued involving the women, but allegedly not the defendant who testified that he first went outside and then went upstairs "to avoid hassling with them." After it became quiet, defendant started to go downstairs, but was said to have been met on the landing by Freda, Pauline, and Anita. Defendant testified that Freda had a knife in her hand and that he struggled with the three women, during which time he grabbed Freda's hand holding the knife and lashed out. Anita, Freda, and Pauline all suffered serious stab wounds. Defendant then took the knife and went back upstairs where he stated that he accidentally stabbed Verna as he was forcibly entering the bathroom. Returning downstairs, he allegedly found Leah kneeling on the floor near the door to the kitchen and told Agnes to "call the cops." The police, who had already been notified, arrived shortly thereafter and found defendant in an upstairs bedroom. Leah was found dead in or near the kitchen.

Defendant was charged with second degree murder for the death of Leah, four counts of assault with a deadly weapon in violation of 18 U.S.C. §§ 1153 and 113(c), and four counts of assault resulting in serious bodily injury in violation of 18 U.S.C. §§ 1153 and 113(f). On May 15, 1981 following a jury trial, defendant was acquitted of the murder charge, but was found guilty of four counts of assault resulting in serious bodily injury, three counts of assault with a dangerous weapon, and one count of assault by striking, beating, or wounding. He was sentenced to forty-five years and six months.

Defendant appealed on the ground that the trial court erred in refusing defendant's request for an intoxication instruction.

We are most troubled by the trial court s refusal to instruct the jury on intoxication as a defense to assault with a deadly weapon on which includes the element of *specific intent* to do bodily harm. Because the charges of assault resulting in serious bodily injury and assault by striking, beating, or wounding do not require more than general intent, the trial court s failure to give an intoxication instruction does not affect defendant's convictions on these counts.

A criminal defendant is entitled to an instruction on a theory of defense "if he makes a timely request for such an instruction, if the request is supported by evidence, and if it sets out a correct declaration of law."

The district court refused to give an intoxication instruction on the ground that there was insufficient evidence to support this theory of defense. We note, however, that there was testimony that defendant and his companions made several stops during the afternoon and evening of New Year's Eve to purchase beer and liquor, and that defendant had "passed out" on the couch at Leah's before Freda and her companions arrived. The evidence further suggests that defendant had been drinking from time to time and perhaps almost continuously during the twenty-four hour period preceding the outbreak of violence at Leah's house. Although defendant did not testify that he was intoxicated, we think the evidence would support a finding that he was in fact intoxicated and that as a result there was a reasonable doubt that he lacked the specific intent to do bodily harm. In view of the policy that "trial judges should be liberal in permitting the defendant's theory of defense to be explained to the jury" [70], we conclude that it was error for the trial court to deny defendant's timely request for an intoxication instruction. Furthermore, because we find that the trier of fact could reasonably have been influenced by the trial court's failure to give such an instruction, we must reverse defendant's convictions on the counts of assault with a deadly weapon and remand for new trial.

VISIBLE INTOXICATION: *CONNER V. DUFFY* (71)

In this case, the question was whether appellants raised a genuine issue of material fact as to "visible intoxication." Appellants alleged error in the trial court's grant of summary judgment to appellees.

William Conner (Conner) was injured when a car driven by Walter Duffy (Duffy), along with several friends, was returning home from a baseball game at Veteran's Stadium in Philadelphia when the accident occurred. When police arrived at the scene, Duffy was taken into custody and charged with Driving Under the Influence (DUI). Conner later brought this negligence suit against Nilon Brothers Enterprises (Nilon Bros.), the concessionaire at the Stadium, and the Philadelphia Phillies baseball team (the Phillies) for serving Duffy while he was visibly intoxicated in violation of the Pennsylvania Liquor Code.

Originally, the City of Philadelphia was named as a defendant in the suit along with Nilon Bros. The City was subsequently dropped and the Phillies were added. After discovery, Nilon Bros. and the Phillies moved for summary judgment which was granted by the trial court.

Our standard of review is clear. Summary judgment is properly granted only when the "pleadings, depositions, answers to interrogatories and admissions on file, together with the affidavits, if any, show that there is no genuine issue as to any material fact and that the moving party is entitled to judgment as a matter of law."

Conner's suit was based primarily on the following section of the Pennsylvania Liquor code, known as the Dram Shop Act:

> It shall be unlawful for any licensee or the board, or any employee, servant or agent of such licensee or of the board, or any other person, to sell, furnish or give any liquor or

malt or brewed beverages or to permit any liquor or malt or brewed beverages to be sold, furnished or given, to any person visibly intoxicated, or to any insane person, or to any minor, or to habitual drunkards, or persons of unknown intemperate habits.

In order for an injured plaintiff to recover for a violation of this act, he must prove that: 1) the tortfeasor was served alcoholic beverages while visibly intoxicated; and 2) this violation of the statute proximately caused his injuries. The trial judge found that Conner could not establish that Duffy was served alcoholic beverages by Nilon Bros., or the Phillies while visibly intoxicated. Conner claimed this finding erroneous and that the record amply supports his claim of Duffy's visible intoxication while at the Stadium. The Phillies organization was made a party to this suit through the involvement of its employees at the ballpark, the Phillies Usherettes. The Usherettes worked a seating area known as the Field Boxes which Duffy and his companion occupied on the day of the accident. Field Box patrons would pay an Usherette for a beer and the Usherette would go to the concession stand to retrieve it. The cost of the beer was the same whether purchased through an Usherette or at the concession stand, though Usherettes would sometimes receive tips from the patrons they served.

A preliminary issue regarding the evidence presented at summary judgment concerns the admissibility of various statements offered by Conner as proof of Duffy's visible intoxication. Specifically, Conner offered the statements of two of Duffy's companions, Charles MacDonald and Cary Moyer, and the written "mental impressions" of Nilon Bros. private investigator, Mark Muth. Mr. Muth interviewed MacDonald and Moyer and wrote a report recording his "impressions" of the interviews. MacDonald also gave two other statements regarding the events in question. The trial judge found that this evidence could not be considered in the motion for summary judgment because the statements were unverified, "not admissions, or the result of depositions and [did] not fall within the category of affidavit."

Conner argued that the statements were incorporated into Nilon Bros.' answers to interrogatories and, therefore, must be considered as part of the record on summary judgment as the statements were "adopted" by Nilon Bros. Both parties rely on *Wilkerson v. Allied Van Lines* (72) for support. Our review of the holding in Wilkerson and the answers to interrogatories cited by Conner lead us to conclude that the references made by Nilon Bros. to the documents they produced for discovery do not constitute an adoption or admission on the part of the Nilon Bros. The evidence, therefore, was properly excluded by the trial court as inappropriate for review on summary judgment.

Conner argued, however, that even if the unverified statements were excluded, there remained ample evidence of visible intoxication to allow the case to proceed to trial. The evidence cited by Conner included Moyer's deposition testimony that beer purchases were made at the Stadium, and that Duffy drove erratically upon exiting the Stadium, the police report detailing the drunken state in which Duffy appeared to the arresting officer approximately one hour after the baseball game (slurred speech and bloodshot eyes), the results of the field sobriety and blood alcohol tests performed at the scene of the accident and at the hospital, and the "relation back" testimony by Conner's expert who opined that based on the blood alcohol test results, Duffy would have appeared intoxicated during the time he was at the Stadium.

Beginning with Moyer's deposition testimony, we encounter some difficulty concluding that Moyer's statements support, rather than contradict Conner's arguments. Moyer plainly testified that Duffy did not appear intoxicated while at the Stadium. As far as erratic driving is concerned, Moyer testified that Duffy was unfamiliar with the roads and so missed an initial turn to enter Interstate 95. As a result, the group had to travel on local roads longer than planned before reaching the highway. Moyer stated that he was never concerned about Duffy's driving, and at no time did Duffy appear incapable of controlling the vehicle. With respect to beer purchases, Moyer simply could not testify to ever seeing Duffy purchase beer from either a concession stand or an Usherette, but suspected that at some point he had. The appellees argued compellingly that Conner failed to offer evidence that Duffy had been served alcoholic beverages at all, by either Nilon Bros. or the Phillies. Moyer could only say that he and his five companions alternately purchased beer for any of those in the group who wanted a beer at that particular time. The nexus between beer purchases by Duffy and his visible intoxication was never established. Indeed, the only certain testimony Moyer gave on this issue was that Duffy did not appear intoxicated while at the Stadium.

Conner's proof of Duffy's visible intoxication therefore depends on the other evidence set out above, namely, Duffy's appearance at the time of his arrest, his blood alcohol level and the expert's relation back testimony. Conner insists that this evidence is insufficient under our holdings in *Couts v. Chion* (73) and *Speicher v. Reda* (74). In *Couts*, the panel was confronted with the question of whether direct eyewitness evidence of visible intoxication was necessary for a civil suit based on a violation of the Dram Shop Act. The evidence in Couts' court consisted of the arresting officer's testimony regarding the driver's visible intoxication at the time of the accident, evidence that the driver consumed a great amount of alcohol while at the bar in question, evidence that the driver drove erratically and without headlights upon leaving the bar, as well as evidence that the driver's blood alcohol level was 0.12 three hours after the accident.

The *Couts* court, in an opinion in which one judge dissented and another concurred in the result, found that this evidence was sufficient to allow the issue of visible intoxication to go to the jury. We are, of course, not bound by the plurality decision in *Couts*. Further, we find significant differences from the instant facts and those in *Couts*, including the lack of erratic driving, the difference in the elapsed time between the blood alcohol testing and the accident, and the fact that there is testimony by Moyer that he and Duffy consumed more beer in the car after leaving the Stadium while on their way home.

We further find that Conner's case cannot rise to the level of establishing a genuine use of material fact simply through the "relation back" testimony of the expert. In *Johnson v. Harris* (75), a panel of this court warned:

> "The Pennsylvania Supreme Court has on various occasions discussed the complexity of 'relation back' testimony and has indicated that it should be used guardedly. We are

accordingly wary of an attempt to create a genuine issue of fact as visible intoxication" based on medical testimony of what the average person's reaction might have been assuming [the driver's] 'probable' blood alcohol concentration."

We agree with the trial court that Conner failed to establish a genuine issue of material fact as to visible intoxication.

Conner offered another theory of liability in addition to the violation of § 4-493. He claimed that the parties also violated § 4-492(15) of the Liquor Code, which prohibits malt or brewed beverage licensees from knowingly selling any malt or brewed beverages to any person engaged in the business of illegally selling liquor or malt or brewed beverages. Conner reasons that by allowing Usherettes to retrieve beer for patrons in the Field Boxes, Nilon Bros. knowingly sold the beer to the Phillies employees who then illegally sold the beer to the patrons.

Putting aside for a moment the fact that such a claim would apply only to Nilon Bros. since the Phillies organization is not a licensee, and the fact that Nilon Bros. claims § 4-492 does not apply to it since it is a "Stadium Licensee" (as defined by § 4-408) and not a brewed or malt beverage licensee, we reject this theory of relief. The agreement between Bros. and the Phillies to allow Usherettes to retrieve beer for Field Box patrons simply does not constitute "knowing" sales to persons engaged in illegal liquor sales. The trial court found that non-licensees who furnish alcohol to an adult who later injures a third party cannot be held liable under the "consumption rule" set out in Klein v. Reisinger (76). In his brief, Conner argues that the "for-profit" service by the Phillies is far different from the circumstances of Klein. We decline to address this aspect of the issue as we find the underlying basis for Conner's theory of recovery, i.e., that Nilon Bros. was selling beer to the Phillies Usherettes who were then illegally selling the beer, meritless.

Order granting summary judgment in favor of appellees was affirmed.

COMMENTARY

Conner v. Duffy acts as a warning to sports stadiums throughout the country that they have a responsibility not to serve alcohol to visibly intoxicated patrons. This is often forgotten by operators or licensees in these environments who mistakenly believe that only bars, restaurants and hotels are sued for violation of the Dram Shop Act. This case is also noteworthy for its emphasis on the phenomenon of "relation back" testimony as referred to by *Johnson v. Harris*. This is now established in Pennsylvania courts and is an issue which should be familiar to everyone involved in the litigation of intoxication.

PROBLEM OF SINGLE BLOOD ALCOHOL READING: CHAPPAQUIDDICK

On the night of 18th, or the early morning hours of the 19th of July, 1969, a car driven by Senator Edward M. Kennedy of Massachusetts took a wrong turn and left the highway on the Dyke Bridge on Chappaquiddick Island, Cape Cod, Massachusetts. The car plunged into the water, and the passenger in the vehicle, a twenty-eight-year-old secretary named Mary Jo Kopechne, was killed.

The part-time medical examiner, Dr. Donald P. Mills, received a telephone call at approximately 9:00 A.M. on the 19th of July informing him of a fatality on Chappaquiddick Island. He proceeded to the Dyke Bridge where he found the body of Ms. Kopechne dressed in a long-sleeved, white shirt, brassiere, black slacks and sandals. Light percussion of the chest produced water from her mouth and pressure on her thorax resulted in water spurting from both her nose and mouth. Foam was seen around her nose. His examination took, at most, ten to fifteen minutes, following which he commented to a police officer that death was due to drowning.

Before leaving the scene of the accident, Dr. Mills was told that this case had a "Kennedy connection" and he informed the undertakers that he was going to contact the district attorney to establish whether or not an autopsy would be necessary. Dr. Mills later testified that after he had called the state police asking them to notify the district attorney, he received a call from a state police lieutenant telling him that no autopsy would be necessary if he was satisfied with the diagnosis of death by drowning. The mortician testified in the same proceeding that Dr. Mills had called him at approximately

12:30 P.M. that Saturday, and told him that no autopsy would be needed.

Mary Jo Kopechne's body was flown from Chappaquiddick Island to Pennsylvania on Sunday, July 20th, and subsequently buried there. No autopsy was ever performed and no one other than Dr. Mills carried out any kind of medical examination. The district attorney at Chappaquiddick later testified that he had called the state police to order an autopsy, but that he had been told that the body had already been removed. In fact, at the time that the district attorney was informed of the findings (approximately 10:00 A.M. on July 20, 1969) the body of Mary Jo Kopechne was still on the island. In proceedings in the Pennsylvania courts several months later, a petition to obtain an exhumation order was denied. This was in spite of the medical examiner for the City of Philadelphia, Dr. Joseph W. Spellman, stating that an autopsy carried out even after many months might "produce evidence that would modify or even completely negate the findings of Dr. Mills that the cause of death was drowning." This position was supported by two other experts, Dr. Cyril H. Wecht and Dr. George Katsas who also warned against the danger of diagnosing death by drowning without an autopsy.

The possibility of severe internal injuries was never excluded, and Dr. Spellman stated in his testimony "It has been my repeated experience that an external examination alone, even if carefully and thoroughly conducted, frequently fails to reveal internal injuries, such as fractured skulls, lesions of the brain, broken necks, broken ribs, ruptured internal organs or natural disease processes." Dr. Katsas also commented that "literally dozens of times every year, we have bodies which will not have a mark on them and which will be found to have a significant pathology internally, by which I mean a pathology which actually was the cause of death."

A sample of blood taken from Ms. Kopechne was found to have a blood alcohol concentration of .097. The Boston Globe quoted Dr. Mills as stating "There was a degree of alcohol, but it was very well down. She was not drunk at the time this happened. She was not drinking immoderately." He was further quoted by the New York Times as saying that the level of alcohol in her blood was "very moderate, very slight, the sort of thing that anyone would have with a couple of drinks before dinner and maybe a highball afterwards." In his book, *The Bridge at Chappaquiddick* (77), Jack Olsen describes a conversation which took place on Sunday, July 20th, between Dr. Mills and the laboratory as follows:

> "Doc, we thought you'd like this information quickly. The alcohol content in the girl's blood was .09%."
>
> "What does that amount to?" Dr. Mills asked.
>
> "Oh, she wasn't really drunk, it sounds like a little social drinking, maybe two or three cocktails and maybe a high-ball, that's all."

These comments about the significance of the blood alcohol concentration in Ms. Kopechne did not take into consideration any report of her actual drinking behavior, what she might have eaten, from what body site the blood sample was taken, or what time her last drink was consumed. It was therefore impossible to know whether her blood alcohol concentration was rising or falling before or after the accident and before her death.

In their book *Intoxication Test Evidence: Criminal and Civil*, Fitzgerald and Hume (78) have posited five basic questions that need to be taken into consideration in evaluating the .09% blood alcohol concentration in this case:

1) Assuming that she did, in fact, have a .09% BAC at the time of the accident, was Dr. Mills justified in concluding, as of the report to him, that Mary Kopechne was not drunk? That she would not have been intoxicated? [No.]

2) Assuming that she did, in fact, have a .09% at the time of the accident, can we determine from that, and from the information available to Dr. Mills, whether she had been drinking moderately or immoderately? [No]

3) Assuming that she did, in fact, have a .09% at the time of her death (which might have been an hour or more after the accident), can we infer from that value, and from the other information available to Mills at that time, what her BAC was an hour or more before her death? [No]

4) Can we, on the information available to Mills or to the laboratory chemist, assume that she indeed did have a 0.09% BAC at her death? [No] Or at the time of the accident? [No] Can we simply assume as a fact that her pre-accident BAC was not affected by drowning, and by the fact that her body was full of water when found? [No]

5) In a case like this, can we simply assume as a fact that the victim suffered no internal injuries, that there were no tears or ruptures of arteries or vessels, that no internal bleeding and fluid replacement took place, and that the integrity of the blood at the site where the sample was collected was unaffected in any way by the accident and her drowning? [No]

COMMENTARY

This case received extensive coverage in the media, and many questions still remain unanswered. Had appropriate questions been raised about the significance of the blood alcohol concentration of .09%, a more accurate understanding of Ms. Kopechne's behavior prior to her death might have been forthcoming.

For example, even if we accept that her BAC at the time of death was .09%, this does not tell us whether the BAC was rising or falling at that time, or whether her BAC was much higher than this sometime during the afternoon and evening, and it had been falling possibly for several hours. Without knowing what her stomach alcohol content was at the time of death, we cannot know whether she had consumed a large quantity of alcohol just before the accident, and that this was only partially absorbed when death occurred. The .09% BAC does not tell us how much alcohol she consumed that afternoon and evening, and it could have been consistent with a much higher intake of alcohol than was assumed to be the case by Dr. Mills. The lesson to be learned here is that a single BAC reading, on its own, does not allow us to make accurate assumptions about the quantity of alcohol consumed.

Without an autopsy shortly after death, it is impossible to know whether Ms. Kopechne died within a few minutes of the car becoming submerged, or whether she survived for several hours. Depending on the position of the car, she could have lived for an appreciable time on trapped air pockets so that the BAC at the time of the accident (assumed inaccurately to be .09%) could have been higher or lower.

This case demonstrates that one needs to be extremely careful in drawing conclusions from a single blood alcohol concentration reading, and that the statements made by Dr. Mills clearly indicated his inexperience in interpreting BAC results. Interestingly, despite the intense media attention, the interpretations of Mary Jo Kopechne's .09% BAC was never questioned or challenged by the various doctors, lawyers, judges or journalists involved in this case.

THE WILLIAM HOLDEN CASE

William Holden, a very well-known and admired actor, was found dead in his Santa Monica apartment on November 16, 1981. The medical examiner of Los Angeles County, Thomas T. Noguchi, M.D., examined the body and postulated that Mr. Holden had slipped on the rug in his apartment while alone and struck his head on a wooden table. He then apparently bled to death, although the presence of a quantity of tissues stained with blood suggested that he might have been conscious for some time and attempted to stop the bleeding.

Dr. Noguchi noted later that while he was supervising the autopsy, he had observed a severe laceration on the forehead and, in his words, "rigor mortis in the limbs of the body and the body condition, including surrounding data as body temperature and decomposition, cloudy eyes and a greenish abdomen, indicated that he had been dead at least four days before he had been found" (79). A sample of blood taken from the body showed a blood alcohol concentration of .22%.

Dr. Noguchi concluded that Holden was "heavily intoxicated" and that his death was accidental, but alcohol-related. He also reported that the blood alcohol concentration of .22% was that at the time of death.

COMMENTARY

This is an example of an intoxication death in which the medical examiner, Dr. Noguchi, should be, and was, severely criticized for his conclusions. Nowhere in his writings did Dr. Noguchi recognize that, after decomposition has begun, and has continued for some length of time, blood alcohol concentrations are highly suspect. It is difficult to believe that Dr. Noguchi did not know that his statement that the blood alcohol level at death was .22% was far from an accurate representation of the facts. It was in fact the policy of his own department to not analyze decomposed bodies for alcohol levels because of highly probable error in the test. He, therefore, had no reliable facts from which to base his conclusion that Holden was "heavily intoxicated" when he fell. Under the circumstances in which the blood was collected and tested, he also had no evidence whatever on which to base the estimated blood alcohol concentration at the time of death.

In his report to the press, Dr. Noguchi also stated that he considered William Holden to be severely intoxicated. By his own admission, and the observation of many others, William Holden was a known chronic alcoholic. He had a prodigious reputation for being able to "hold his liquor and his tolerance to liquor had been very obvious even in a heavy drinking community, such as the one to which he belonged. It was said that Holden was able to drink more "cardtables" than any other actor, a "cardtable" being a California drink named because "after two, your legs fold under you upon trying to stand," As we have seen, such drinkers have significant tolerance to alcohol, and several studies have demonstrated that some individuals with BACs well above 0.20% demonstrate no evidence of alcohol intoxication. Dr. Noguchi ignored these data and gave an opinion that was largely guesswork.

Dr. Noguchi stated that when he viewed the scene of the death, he had found an empty quart-bottle of vodka in the trash can, and a partially empty bottle on a counter. It is not known, however, whether the actor drank any, some, or all of the vodka. Without knowing any of these facts, Dr. Noguchi was only too ready to release to the press his unscientific conclusions regarding Mr. Holden's death.

*****

This book is not meant to be a comprehensive medical or legal text but has attempted to describe some basic facts about the physiology of alcohol, the psychosocial consequences of its abuse and details of the author's experience in helping to litigate cases involving alcohol intoxication. There are also descriptions of significant legal cases which helped to demonstrate some of the complex legal issues involved in various aspects of intoxication.

REFERENCES

1. Clum FD: Inebriety: Its Causes, Its Results, Its Remedy, 3rd edition. Philadelphia, JP Lippincott, 1892

2. Victor M, Adams RD: The effect of alcohol on the nervous system. Res Publ Assoc Nerv Ment Dis 1953; 32:526-573

3. Jaffe JH: Drug Addition and Drug Abuse. The Pharmacological Basis of Therapeutics, 6th edition. Edited by Gilman AG, Goodman LS, Gilman A. New York, Macmillan, 1980; 535-584

4. Dubowski KM: Absorption, distribution and elimination of alcohol: highway safety aspects. J Stud Alcohol (supplement), July 1985; 10:98-108

5. American Psychiatric Association: Diagnostic and Statistical Manual of Mental Disorders (4th ed. rev.). Washington, D.C., 1994

6. National Council on Alcoholism: Criteria for the diagnosis of alcoholism. Ann Intern Med 1972; 77:249-258

7. Edwards G, Gattoni F, Hensman C: Correlates of alcohol-dependence scores in a prison population. O J Stud Alcohol 1972; 33:417-419

8. Guze SB, Tuason VB, Gatfield PD, Stewart MA, Picken B: Psychiatric illness and crime with particular reference to alcoholism: a study of 233 criminals. J Nerv Ment Dis 1962; 134:512-521

9. Seltzer ML: The Michigan Alcoholism Screening Test (MAST): the quest for a new diagnostic instrument. Am J Psychiat 1971; 127:1653-1658

10. Mortimer RG, Filkins LD, Kerlan MW, Lower JS: Psychometric identification of problem drinkers. O J Stud Alcohol 1963; 34:1332-1335

11. National Council on Alcoholism: Criteria for the diagnosis of alcoholism. Ann Intern Med 1972; 77:249-258

12. Linnoila M, Virkkunen M, Scheinin M, Rimon R, Goodwin FK: Low cerebrospinal fluid 5-hydroxyindole acetic acid concentra-

tion differentiates impulsive from nonimpulsive violent behavior. Life Sci 1983; 33:26:2609-2614

13. Abel EL, Zeidenberg P: Age, alcohol and violent death: a postmortem study, J Stud Alcohol 1985; 46:3:228-231

14. Roy A, Virkkunen M, Linnoila M: Reduced central serotenin turnover in a subgroup of alcoholics? Prog Neuropsychopharmacol Biol Psychiatry 1987; 11:173-177

15. Winslow JT, Ellingboe J, Miczek KA: Effects of alcohol on aggressive behavior in squirrel monkeys: influence of testosterone and social context. Psychopharm 1988; 95:350-353

16. Graham J: Vessels of Rage, Engines of Power. Aculeus Press, Inc., Lexington, 1994

17. American Psychiatric Association: Diagnostic and Statistical Manual of Mental Disorders (3rd ed. rev.). Washington, D.C., 1980

18. National Center for Statistics and Analysis: Drunk Driving Facts. Washington, D.C., National Highway Traffic Safety Administration , 1988

19. Fine EW, Scoles P, Mulligan MJ: Under the influence: characteristics and drinking practices of persons arrested the first time for drunk driving, with treatment implications. Public Health Reports 90:424-429, 1975.

20. National Council on Alcoholism: Criteria for the diagnosis of alcoholism. Ann Intern Med 1972; 77:249-258

21. Fine EW, Steer RA, Scoles PE: Relationship between blood alcohol concentration and self-reported drinking behavior. J Stud Alcohol, March 1978; 39:3:466-472

22. National Institute on Alcohol Abuse and Alcoholism: Alcohol Alert. No. 25 PH351, July, 1993

23. Shelton J, Hollister L, Golka E: Quantifying alcoholic impairment. Mod Med, Nov. 17, 1969; 5:188-189

24. Wolk AA, Attorney, Aviation Law, 1712 Locust St., Philadelphia, PA, Personal communication, 1994

25. Wright SJ: SOS: alcohol, drugs and boating. Alc Health and Res World 1985; 9:4:28-33

26. Howland J, Hingson R: Alcohol as a risk factor for drownings: a review of the literature (1950-1985). Accid Anal Prev 1988; 20:19-25

27. Hingson R, Howland J: Alcohol as a risk factor for injury or death resulting from accidental falls: a review of the literature. J Stud Alcohol 1987; 48:212-219

28. Honkanen R, Ertama L, Kuosmanen P, Linnoila M, Alk, A, Vessiri T: The role of alcohol in accidental falls. J Stud Alcohol 1983; 44:231-245

29. Howland J, Hingson R: Alcohol as a risk factor for injuries or death due to fires and burns: review of the literature. Pub Health Rep 1987; 102:475-483

30. Schmidt W, deLint J: Causes of deaths of alcoholics. Quart J Stud Alc 1972; 33:171-185

31. Combs-Orme T, Taylor JR, Scott EB, Holmes SJ: Violent deaths among alcoholics: a descriptive study. J Stud Alc 1983; 44:6:938-944

32. Waller JA: Nonhighway injury fatalities-I. The roles of alcohol and problem drinking, drugs and medical impairment. J Chronic Dis 1972; 25:33-45

33. Howland J, Hingson R: Alcohol as a risk factor for injuries or death due to fires and burns: review of the literature. Pub Health Rep 1987; 102:475-483

34. Smith CW: Intoxication as a defense to a criminal charge in Pennsylvania. Dickinson Law Review 1971; 76:15

35. Aristotle: The Nicomachean Ethics III, 5. Translated by Ross D. Oxford University Press, 1980

36. d'Orban T: Drugs and alcohol: the psychiatrist as expert witness in court. British Journal of Addiction 1986; 81:631-639

37. Van Hasselt VB, Morrison RL, Bellack AS: Alcohol use in wife abusers and their spouses. Addict Behav 1985; 10:127-135

38. Leonard KE, Jacob T: Alcohol, alcoholism, and family violence, in Handbook of Family Violence. Edited by Van Hasselt VB, Morrison RL, Bellack AS, Hersen M. New York, Plenum, 1988; 383-406

39. Bland R, Orn H: Family Violence and Psychiatric Disorder. Can J Psychiatry 1986; 31:129-137

40. Director of Public Prosecutions v. Bearh. A.C. 479, 1920

41. Dram Shop Act of May 8, 1854 (39), P.L. 663, No. 648, Commonwealth of Pennsylvania

42. Fink v. Carman, 40 Pa. 95 (1861)

43. Davies v. Knight, 146 Pa., 610, 23A. 320 (1892)

44. McCusker v. Quinn, 26 Pa. D. 499 (1917)

45. Pennsylvania Liquor Code, Act of April 12, 1951, Section 4-493; 47 P.S. 4-497

46. Pennsylvania Liquor Code, Act of April 12, 1951, Section 4-493; 47 P.S. 4-497

47. Fine EW, Gemberling MS: The Dram Shop Act in Pennsylvania: strategies for the defense. American Journal of Forensic Psychiatry 1992; 13:3:5-13

48. Congini v. Portersville Valve Company, 504 Pa. 157, 470 A. 2d 515 (1983)

49. Jefferis v. Commonwealth of Pennsylvania and Theta Chi Fraternity, 537 A. 2d 355 Pa. Super. (1988)

50. Fasset v. Villanova Chapter of Delta Kappa Epsilon and its Individual Members, et al., 807 F 2d 1150 3rd Cir. (1986)

51. Alumni Association v. Sullivan, 524 Pa. 356, 572 A. 2d, 1209 (1990)

52. Bradshaw v. Rawlins, 612 F 2d 135 3rd Cir. (1979)

53. Millard v. Osbourne, 416 Pa. Super. 474, 611 A. 2d 715 (1992)

54. Goldberg v. Delta Tau Delta, 418 Pa. Super. 207, 613 A. 2d 1250 (1992)

55. Kapres v. Heller, 417 Pa. Super. 371, 612 A. 2d 987 (1992)

56. State v. Downie, 117 NJ 450, 569 Ad 242 (1990)

57. Roberts v. People, 19 Mich. 401 (1870)

58. Robinson PH: Criminal Law Defenses, Vol 1. St. Paul, West Publishing Co., 1984; 302-303

59. State v. Alie, 82 W.Va. 601, 96 SE. 1011 (1918)

60. People v. Penman, 271 111. 82, 110 N.E. 894 (1915)

61. Carbutt, Roberts v. People, 19 Mich. 401 (1870)

62. Boettcher MD: Voluntary intoxication: a defense to specific intent crimes. University of Detroit Law Review 1988; 65:33:33-71

63. Commonwealth of Pennsylvania v. Randy Joe REIFF, Appellant (Supreme Court of Pennsylvania, Submitted March 3, 1980, Decided April 25, 1980)

64. Commonwealth v. Kichline, 468 PA 265, 361 A.2d 282 (1975)

65. Commonwealth of Pennsylvania v. Anthony Lee Cessna, Appellant (Superior Court of Pennsylvania; Argued Dec. 3, 1987; Filed Feb. 1, 1988)

66. Commonwealth v. Stark, 363 PA Super. 356, 526 A.2d 383 (1987)

67. Commonwealth v. Verdekal, 351 PA Super, 412, 506 A.2d 415 (1986)

68. Commonwealth v. Moore, 473 PA 169, 373 A.2d 1101 (1977).

69. United States of America (Appellee) v. Leighton Lee Fay (February 6; United States Court of Appeals,; Eighth Circuit; Submitted Nov. 12, 1981; Decided Dec. 30, 1981)

70. United States v. Brown, 540 F 23 364, 381 (8th Cir. 1976),

71. Conner v. Duffy (Appellants) v. Walter A. Duffy and City of Philadelphia and the Phillies (Appellees) (Appeal in the Court of Common Pleas of Delaware County Civil, No. 85-10182)

72. Wilkerson v. Allied Van Lines, 360 PA Super. 523, 521 A. 2d 25 (1987, appeal dismissed, 518 PA 61, 540 A. 2d 265, cert. denied. 488 U.S. 827 (1988),

73. Couts v. Chion, 281 PA Super 135, 421 A, 2d 11.84 (1.980)

74. Speicher v. Reda, 290 PA Super. 168, 434 A. 2d 183 (1981.).

75. Johnson v. Harris, 419 PA Super 541, 615 A.2d 771 (1992),

76. Klein v. Reisinger, 504 PA 141, 470 A.2d 507 (1983).

77. Olsen J: The Bridge at Chappaquiddick. New York, Ace Books, 1970

78. Fitzgerald E, Hume D: Intoxication Test Evidence: Criminal and Civil. Boston, Clark and Boardman, Lawyers Cooperative Publ. Co., 1987

79. Noguchi TT: Postmortem findings re: William Holden, in Intoxication Test Evidence: Criminal and Civil. Edited by Fitzgerald E, Hume D. Boston, Clark and Boardman, Lawyers Cooperative Publ. Co., 1987

SUGGESTED FURTHER READINGS

Alcohol and the Impaired Driver: a Manual on the Medicolegal Aspects of Chemical Tests. Committee on Medicolegal Problems, American Medical Association, Chicago, 1968

Fine EW, Scoles P: Alcohol, alcoholism and highway safety. Public Health Reviews 1974; 3:423-436

Fine EW, Scoles P: Secondary prevention of alcoholism using a population of offenders arrested for driving while intoxicated, in Work in Progress on Alcoholism. Annals of the New York Academy of Sciences, Vol. 273, 1976; 637-645

Goodman LS, Gilman AG: The Pharmacological Basis of Therapeutics. 6th Edition. New York, Macmillan, 1980; chapter 18

Lishman WA: Organic Psychiatry: The Psychological Consequences of Cerebral Disorder. Blackwell Scientific Publications, 1978

U.S. Department of Health and Human Services: Sixth Special Report to the U.S. Congress on Alcohol and Health, DHSS Pub. No. (ADM) 87-1519. Supt. of Docs., U.S. Government Printing Office, Washington, D.C., 1987

U.S. Department of Health and Human Services: Seventh Special Report to the U.S. Congress on Alcohol and Health. ADM 281-88-0002. Supt. of Docs., U.S. Government Printing Office, Washington, D.C., 1990

Wolfgang ME: Patterns of Criminal Homicide. Philadelphia, University of Pennsylvania, 1958

❧ *NOTES* ❧

❧ NOTES ❧

❧ *NOTES* ❧

❧ NOTES ❧